under
cover

60 Afghans to Knit and Crochet

under cover

60 Afghans to Knit and Crochet

Sixth&Spring Books
New York

Editorial Director
Trisha Malcolm

Art Director
Christy Hale

Cover Design
Chi Ling Moy

Technical Editor
Carla Scott

Copy Editor
Pat Harste

Yarn Editor
Veronica Manno

Photographer
Dan Howell

Stylist
Laura Maffeo

Intern
Susan Hoover

Book Division Manager
Michelle Lo

Production Manager
David Joinnides

Publisher, Sixth&Spring Books
Art Joinnides

We have made every effort to ensure the accuracy of the contents of this
publication. We are not responsible for any human or typographical error.

Library of Congress Cataloging-in-Publication Data
Under cover : 60 afghans to knit and crochet.
     p. cm.
ISBN 1-931543-59-3
1. Afghans (Coverlets) 2. Knitting—Patterns. 3. Crocheting—Patterns.
TT825.U53 2004
746.43'0437--dc22

                                                                    2003070373

Manufactured in China
1 3 5 7 9 10 8 6 4 2

First Edition

contents

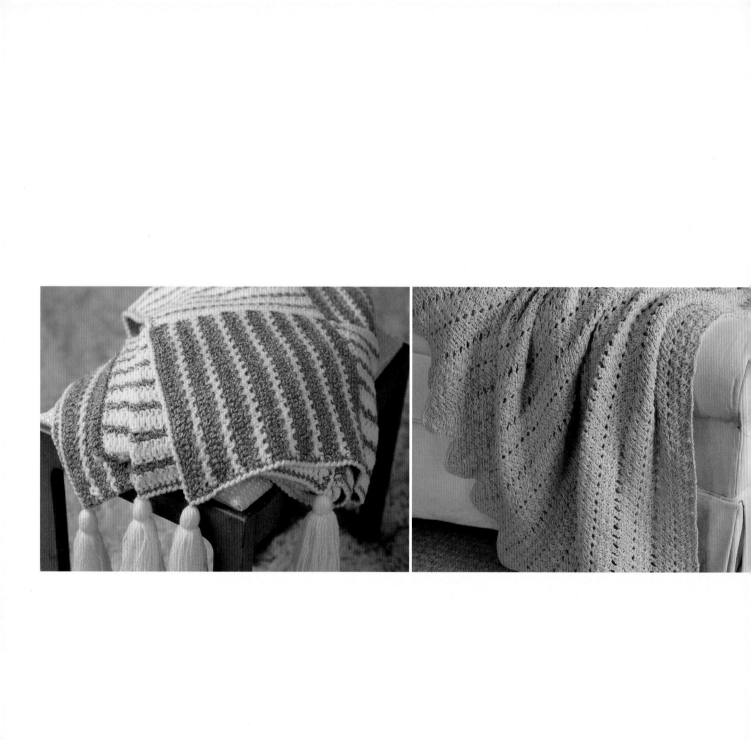

easy stripes

These original throws transform a basic design
from ordinary to extraordinary.

simply casual

easy

finished measurements

46" x 57½"/117 x 146cm

gauge

13 sts and 10 rows to 4"/10cm over pat st using size J/10 (6mm) crochet hook.
TAKE TIME TO CHECK YOUR GAUGE.

motif I

(make 10)

With A, ch 37.

Row 1 (WS) Sc in 2nd ch from hook and in each ch across—36 sts. Turn.

Row 2 Ch 3 (counts as I dc), sk first sc, I dc in each sc to end of row, changing to B at end of last dc. Turn.

Row 3 With B, ch 1, I sc in first dc, *ch 1, sk next dc, I sc in next dc; rep from * across, end with I sc in top of turning ch. Turn.

Row 4 Ch 1, I sc in first sc, *ch 1, sk next sc, I sc in next ch-1 sp; rep from * to last sc, end I sc in last sc, changing to A at end of last sc. Turn.

Row 5 With A, ch 1, I sc in each sc and ch-1 sp to end of row. Turn.

Row 6 Rep row 2.

Rep rows 3-6 for pat st until motif measures approx 11"/28cm from beg, end with row 6. Fasten off.

motif II

(make 10)

Rep as for motif I, using B instead of A and A instead of B.

finishing

Referring to placement diagram, sew motifs into 4 strips of 5 motifs each, alternating motif I with motif II and rotating motif II for vertical stripes. Sew 4 strips together.

Edging

Rnd 1 With RS facing, join A with a sl st in any corner, ch 1, work 3 sc in same st as sl st, sc evenly around, working 3 sc in each corner. Join with a sl st in first sc. Fasten off.

Rnd 2 Join B with a sl st in any corner, ch 1, working from left to right, sc in each st round. Join with a sl st in first sc. Fasten off.

Tassels

(make 4)

Wind B 40 times around cardboard. Cut yarn leaving a long end and thread end into yarn needle. Sl needle through all lps and tie tightly. Remove cardboard and wind yarn tightly around lps 1"/2.5cm below fold. Fasten securely. Cut through rem lps and trim ends evenly.

Sew a tassel to each corner.

materials

Denimstyle by Bernat®, 3½oz/100g, each approx 196yd/179m (acrylic/cotton)
6 balls in #3006 canvas (B)
5 balls in #3117 stonewash (A)

Size J/10 (6mm) crochet hook
OR SIZE TO OBTAIN GAUGE

7½"/19cm square of cardboard

Yarn needle

placement diagram

II	I	II	I
I	II	I	II
II	I	II	I
I	II	I	II
II	I	II	I

waffled coverlet

easy

finished measurements

52" x 69"/132 x 175cm

gauge

16 sts and 12 rows to 4"/10cm over pat st using larger hook.
TAKE TIME TO CHECK YOUR GAUGE.

coverlet

With larger hook, ch 149.
Row 1 Dc in 4th ch from hook and in each ch across. Ch 1, turn.
Row 2 Working through front lps, sc in each st across. Ch 1, turn.
Row 3 Sc in back lp of first sc, *dc in next sc inserting hook from below up through front lp of previous row, yo, complete dc, sc in next sc in back lp; rep from * across, end with a sc. Ch 1, turn.
Rows 4 and 5 With A, rep rows 2 and 3.
Rows 6 and 7 With B, rep rows 2 and 3.
Rows 8 and 9 With C, rep rows 2 and 3.
Rows 10 and 11 With B, rep rows 2 and 3.

Rows 12–15 With D, rep rows 2 and 3.
Rows 16 and 17 With B, rep rows 2 and 3.
Rows 18 and 19 With C, rep rows 2 and 3.
Rows 20 and 21 With B, rep rows 2 and 3.
Rows 22–25 With A, rep rows 2 and 3.
Rep rows 2-21 8 times more, then rows 2-5 once more. Fasten off.

finishing

Edging

Rnd 1 From RS with smaller hook, join A at bottom RH corner. Work 3 dc in bottom of st, keeping work flat, work dc at end of rows to top corner, 3 dc in ch 1 at top, dc in back lp of sts, across row, 3 dc in sc, dc at end of rows to last st of row 1, 3 dc. Join in first ch of foundation. Fasten off. **Rnd 2** Join B in back lp of any st with a sc, work sc in back lp of each st and 3 sc in center st of each corner. Fasten off. **Rnd 3** Join C in any st, ch 3, working through both lps of st, dc around, working 3 dc at center st of each corner. Join. Fasten off. **Rnd 4** Join B in back lp of any st with sc, sc around working 3 sc in corners or rep rnd 2. **Rnd 5** With A rep rnd 3. Work 2 dc in each of 3 center sts at corners. Fasten off.

materials

Wintuk® by Caron®, 3½oz/100g skeins, each approx 213yd/195m (acrylic)
7 skeins in #3001 white (B)
4 skeins each in #3021 oatmeal (A) and #3044 nutmeg (C)
3 skeins in #3025 baby pink (D)

Size H/8 and I/9 (5 and 5.5mm) crochet hooks OR SIZE TO OBTAIN GAUGE

crochet ripple

materials

*Perfect Match® by Caron®, 8oz/226g
skeins, each approx 400yd/366m (acrylic)
5 skeins in #7747 powder blue (A)
4 skeins in #7707 soft peach (B)*

---

*Size J/10 (6mm) crochet hook
OR SIZE TO OBTAIN GAUGE*

intermediate

finished measurements

60" x 76"/152.5 x 193cm

gauge

22 sts between points to 4"/10 and 8 rows to 6"/15cm over pat st using size J/10 (6mm) crochet hook.
TAKE TIME TO CHECK YOUR GAUGE.

afghan

With A, ch 319 for base chain.

Row 1 Dc in 5th ch from hook, 1 dc in next ch, *ch 2, sk 2 ch, 1 dc in each of next 2 ch, ch 2, sk 2 ch, 1 dc in next ch, work 1 dc, ch 2, 1 dc all in next ch for ascending point, 1 dc in next ch, [ch 2, sk 2 ch, 1 dc in each of next 2 ch] twice, sk next 2 ch for descending point, 1 dc in each of next 2 ch; rep from * across, ending last rep with sk 1 ch, 1 dc in last ch—there are 14 full descending points with ½ point at each end. Ch 3, turn.

Row 2 (RS) Drawing up lp of each dc to ¾"/2cm, sk first 3 dc, *[working over ch on previous row, work 1 dc in each of 2 sk ch of base-ch, ch 2, sk 2 dc] twice, work 2 dc, ch 2, 2 dc all in ch-2 sp of ascending point, [ch 2, sk 2 dc, working over ch, work 1 dc in each of 2 sk ch of base-ch] twice, sk next 4 dc of descending point (do not ch 2 between dc's over point); rep from * across, ending last rep with sk last 2 dc, 1 dc in top of beg-ch. Mark this row as RS. Ch 3, turn.

Row 3 Drawing up lp of each dc to ¾"/2cm, sk first 3 dc, *[working over ch, work 1 dc in each of 2 sk dc on previous row, ch 2, sk 2 dc] twice, work 2 dc, ch 2, 2 dc all in ch-2 sp of ascending point, [ch 2, sk 2 dc, working over ch, work 1 dc in each of 2 sk dc] twice, sk 4 dc of descending point; rep from * across, ending last rep with sk last 2 dc, 1 dc in 3rd ch of turning-ch. Ch 3, turn. Rep row 3 for pat st.

Rows 4-7 With A, work 4 rows more, working to within last dc of row 7; to change color, yo, sk last 2 dc, insert hook in 3rd ch of turning-ch, yo and draw up a lp, yo and draw through 2 lps only, draw a lp of B through last 2 A lps on hook. Cut A and with B, ch 3, turn. Beg first set of stripes.

Row 8 (RS) With B, work across, changing to A in last dc. Cut B and with A, ch 3, turn.

Row 9 With A, work across changing to B in last dc. Cut A and with B, ch 3, turn.

Rows 10-15 Rep rows 8 and 9, 3 times more, changing to B in last dc of row 15. There should be 4 B stripes and 4 A stripes. With B, ch 3, turn.

Rows 16-22 With B, work 7 rows, changing to A in last dc of row 22. With A, ch 3, turn. Beg second set of stripes.

Rows 23-30 Beg with A, work 8 rows alternating colors every row, changing to A in last dc of 4th B stripe. With A, ch 3, turn.

Rows 31-37 With A work 7 rows, changing to B in last dc of row 37. With B, ch 3, turn. Rep rows 8-37 twice more. Do not change colors at end of row 37 on second rep. With A, ch 1, turn.

Finishing row (RS) Working dc's in usual manner, with A, draw up a lp in each of first 2 dc, yo and draw through all 3 lps on hook for dec, *1 sc in next dc, [working over ch, work 1 dc in each of 2 sk dc, 1 sc in each of next 2 dc] twice,

(continued on page 135)

autumnal harvest

finished measurements

48" x 69"/122 x 175cm

gauge

12 sts to 4"/10cm and 8 rows to 5"/12.5cm over pat st using size I/9 (5.5mm) crochet hook. TAKE TIME TO CHECK YOUR GAUGE.

afghan

With A, ch 196.
Row 1 Sc in 2nd ch from hook and in each ch across—195 sc. Ch 3, turn.
Row 2 *Work 2 dc in next sc, sk 1 sc; rep from * across ending sk next sc, dc in last dc, changing to B. Ch 3, turn.
Row 3 Sk next dc, 2 dc between sk dc and next dc, *2 dc between next set of 2 dc, rep from * across ending dc in top of beg ch. Change to C. Ch 3, turn.

Row 4 With C, rep row 3.
Row 5 With A, rep row 3.
Row 6 With C, rep row 3.
Row 7 With B, rep row 3.
Rows 8 and 9 With A, rep row.
Rep rows 2-9 9 times more, then rows 2-8 once.
Last row With A, work 1 row sc. Fasten off.

finishing

Edging
Rnd 1 Join C in top right corner, ch 3, 2 dc in same st, dc in each st to next corner, 3 dc in corner, (2 dc in end of next row, 1 dc in end of next row) to bottom left corner, work other 2 sides to correspond. Join in top of ch-3. Ch 3, turn.
Rnd 2 Work dc in each dc and 3 dc in each corner dc. Join. Fasten off. Turn. **Rnd 3** Join A in center dc in any corner, ch 3, 5 dc in same st, *sk 1 dc, 2 dc in next st; rep from * to next corner, work 6 dc in center dc; rep from * around. Join. Fasten off.

materials

Natura One Pound® Rainbow Dreams by Caron®, 10oz/285g skeins, each approx 505yd/462m (acrylic)
3 skeins in color of your choice (A)
Natura One Pound® by Caron®, 16oz/456g skeins, each approx 846yd/774m (acrylic)
1 skein each in #0549 sunflower (B) and #0589 cream (C)

Size I/9 (5.5mm) crochet hook
OR SIZE TO OBTAIN GAUGE

fantail fantasy

easy

finished measurements

50" x 58"/127 x 147.5cm

gauge

Top of fan to top of next fan to 2½"/6.5cm over pat st using size H/8 (5mm) crochet hook
TAKE TIME TO CHECK YOUR GAUGE.

stitch glossary

Fan
Work (3 dc, ch 1, 3 dc) in ch or st.
V st
Work (1 hdc, ch 1, 1 hdc) in ch or st.

afghan

With A, ch 241.
Row 1 Sc in 2nd ch from hook, sc in next ch, *sk 3 ch, work Fan in next ch, sk 3 ch, 1 sc in next ch**, ch 1, sk 1, sc in next ch; rep from * ending last rep at **, sc in last ch. Turn.
Row 2 Ch 2, 1 hdc in first st, *ch 3, sc in ch-1 sp of Fan, ch 3, **work V st in next sp, rep from * ending last rep at **, 2 hdc in last sc. Turn.
Row 3 Ch 2, 2 dc in first st, *sc in next ch-3 sp, ch 1, sc in next ch-3 sp, **work a Fan in ch-1 sp of V st; rep from *, ending last rep at **, 4 dc in top of turning ch. Turn.

Row 4 Ch 1, sc in first st, *ch 3, V st in next sp, ch 3, 1 sc in ch-1 sp of next Fan; rep from *, ending last rep in top of turning ch. Turn.
Row 5 Ch 1, sc in first st, *sc in next ch-3 sp, Fan in ch-1 sp of V st, sc in next ch-3 sp, ch 1; rep from *, ending sc in last sc.
Rep rows 2-5 for pat st working color sequence as foll: first 4 rows A, 1 row B, 3 rows A, 1 row B, *7 rows A, 1 row B, 7 rows A, 1 row B, 3 rows A, 1 row B; rep from * 5 times, end 4 rows A.

finishing

Edging

With A, sc along top and bottom edges.
Rnd 1 Join B at top left corner, ch 6, dc in bottom of Fan st, *ch 3, dc in bottom of V st, ch 3, dc in Fan st; rep from * across, work (dc, ch 2, dc, ch 2, dc) in corner, [ch 3, sk 3 sc, dc] along bottom edge. Work 2 other sides working in ch-1 of Fan, end dc, ch 2, twice at corner. Join with a sl st in first ch of ch-6. **Rnd 2** Ch 3, work 3 dc in next sp, dc in next st to corner work (dc in dc, 2 dc in sp, 3 dc, 2 dc in sp, dc) at corner; cont in this manner around. Join with a sl st in 3rd ch of ch-3. **Rnd 3** Ch 1, sc in same st, ch 4, sk 2 dc, sc in next st around, working [sc, ch 4, sk 1] 3 times at corners. Join with a sl st in beg sc. **Rnd 4** Sl st in ch-4 sp, ch 3, work (2 dc, ch 1, 3 dc) in same sp, *sc in next sp, work (3 dc, ch 1, 3 dc) in next sp; rep from * around. Join with a sl st in beg sl st. Fasten off.

materials

Simply Soft® by Caron®, 3oz/85g skeins, each approx 163yd/150m (acrylic)
12 skeins in #9703 bone (A)
6 skeins in #9702 off white (B)

Size H/8 (5mm) crochet hook
OR SIZE TO OBTAIN GAUGE

renaissance throw

finished measurements

45" x 66"/114.5 x 167.5cm (including fringe)

gauge

8 sts and 4 ch-1 sps, and 8 rows to 4"/10cm over dc using size J/10 (6mm) crochet hook.
TAKE TIME TO CHECK YOUR GAUGE.

notes

1 Beg and end each color change with 6"/15cm length.
2 When adding fringe at end of afghan, include these 6"/15cm lengths when joining tassel to end of that row.

afghan

With A (leaving 6"/15cm length at beg), ch 175.
Row 1 Dc in 4th ch from hook, dc in next ch, *sk next ch, ch 1, dc in next 2 chs; rep from * across. Ch 3, turn.

Row 2 Dc in next st, *ch 1, sk next st, dc in next 2 sts; rep from * across. Fasten off, leaving 6"/15cm length yarn. Turn.
Row 3 Join B with an sc in first st, sc in next st, *ch 3, sc in back lp of first ch (picot made), sk next ch, sc in next 2 sts; rep from * across. Fasten off. Turn.
Row 4 Join A with a sl st in first st, ch 3, dc in next st, *ch 1, sk next picot, dc in next 2 sts; rep from * across. Ch 3, turn.
Rows 5 and 6 Dc in next st, *ch 1, sk next st, dc in next 2 sts; rep from * across. Turn. At end of row 6, fasten off.
Rows 7-81 Rep rows 3-6.

finishing

Fringe
For each fringe, cut 3 strands 12"/30.5cm long. Hold all 3 strands together and fold in half. Insert hook in end of row, pull fold through, pull ends of strands through fold, then tighten. Matching yarn of each fringe to row you are working in, place one fringe in each end of all rows. Trim ends evenly.

materials

Perfect Match® by Caron®, 8oz/229g skeins, each approx 400yd/366m (acrylic)
4 skeins in #7730 deep violet (A)
3 skeins in #7744 lilac (B)

Size J/10 (6mm) crochet hook
OR SIZE TO OBTAIN GAUGE

sunset stripes

easy

finished measurements

36" x 54"/91.5 x 137cm (not including border)

gauge

8½ sts to 4"/10cm over pat st using size P/15 (10mm) crochet hook.
TAKE TIME TO CHECK YOUR GAUGE.

stitch glossary

Ssc2 (Spike sc 2 rows below)
Insert hook in next st 2 rows below, yo, draw lp through and up to height of current row, complete sc.

afghan

(multiple of 4 sts plus 3)
With A, ch 76.
Row 1 With A, sc in 2nd ch from hook and in each ch across—75 sts.
Row 2 Ch 1, turn; sc in each sc across.
Rows 3 and 4 With B, rep row 2.
Rows 5 and 6 With C, rep row 2.
Row 7 With D, sc in each of first 3 sts, *Ssc2 in next st, sc in each of next 3 sts; rep from * across.
Row 8 With D, rep row 2.
Row 9 With C, sc in first sc, *Ssc2 in next sc, sc in each of next 3 sc; rep from *, end last rep sc in last sc.

Row 10 With C, rep row 2.
Rows 11 and 12, 15 and 16 With A, rep rows 7 and 8.
Rows 13 and 14 With B, rep rows 9 and 10.
Rows 17 and 18 With C, rep rows 9 and 10.
Rows 19 and 20 With D, rep rows 7 and 8.
Rows 21- 38 Cont in sc only (row 2) in color sequence as foll : 2 rows C, 2 rows B, 2 rows A, 4 rows D, 4 rows C and 4 rows D. Rep rows 1-38 for 3 times, then work rows 1-26. Fasten off.

finishing

Border
Rnd 1 Join C in top right corner and *work 73 sc evenly spaced across short edge, work 3 sc in corner; work 106 sc evenly spaced along side edge work 3 sc in corner; rep from * once more, join with sl st to beg sc. **Rnd 2** Ch 1, work 1 rnd sc, working 3 sc in each corner. Fasten off C. **Rnd 3** Join A in any corner, *(sc, ch 2, sc) in corner st, (ch 1, sk 1, sc in next st) to corner, ch 1; rep from * (adjusting sts as needed), ch 1 and sl st to beg sc. Fasten off A. **Rnd 4** Join D in first sc of any corner, ch 3 (counts as 1 dc), dc, (ch 4, sl st in first ch from hook)—picot made, 2 dc in same space, (2 dc, picot, 2 dc) in next corner sc—group made; counting the ch-1's in rnd 3 as a st, work a group in every 3rd st and work corners with a group in each sc of corner as above, adjusting sts as needed, end sk 2 sts, join with sl st to beg ch. Fasten off.

materials

Chunky★USA by Lion Brand Yarn Co.,
4oz/113g skeins, each approx
155yd/142m (acrylic)
4 skeins in #099 fisherman (C)
3 skeins in #138 crimson (D)
2 skeins each in #152 skyscraper grey (A)
and #100 snowcap white (B)

Size P/15 (10mm) crochet hook
OR SIZE TO OBTAIN GAUGE

chunky comfort

finished measurements

36" x 54"/91.5 x 137cm (without border)

gauge

8½ sts to 4"/10cm over pat st using size P/15 (10mm) crochet hook.
TAKE TIME TO CHECK YOUR GAUGE.

stitch glossary

Ssc2 (Spike sc 2 rows below)
Insert hook in next st 2 rows below, yo, draw lp through and up to height of current row, complete sc.

afghan

(multiple of 4 sts plus 3)
With A, ch 76.
Row 1 With A, sc in 2nd ch from hook and in each ch across—75 sts.
Row 2 Ch 1, turn; sc in each sc across.
Rows 3 and 4 With B, rep row 2.
Rows 5 and 6 With C, rep row 2.
Row 7 With D, sc in each of first 3 sts, *Ssc2 in next st, sc in each of next 3 sts; rep from * across.
Row 8 With D, rep row 2.
Row 9 With C, sc in first sc, *Ssc2 in next sc, sc in each of next 3 sc; rep from *, end last rep sc in last sc.
Row 10 With C, rep row 2.
Rows 11 and 12, 15 and 16 With A, rep rows 7 and 8.
Rows 13 and 14 With B, rep rows 9 and 10.
Rows 17 and 18 With C, rep rows 9 and 10.
Rows 19 and 20 With D, rep rows 7 and 8.
Rows 21- 38 Cont in sc only (row 2) and work in color sequence as foll: 2 rows C, 2 rows B, 2 rows A, 4 rows D, 4 rows C and 4 rows D. Rep rows 1-38 for 3 times, then work rows 1-26. Fasten off.

finishing

Border
Rnd 1 Join C in top right corner and *work 73 sc evenly spaced across short edge, work 3 sc in corner; work 106 sc evenly spaced along side edge work 3 sc in corner; rep from * once more, join with sl st to beg sc. **Rnd 2** Ch 1, work 1 rnd sc, working 3 sc in each corner. Fasten off C. **Rnd 3** Join A in any corner, *(sc, ch 2, sc) in corner st, (ch 1, sk 1, sc in next st) to corner, ch 1; rep from * (adjusting sts as needed), ch 1 and sl st to beg sc. Fasten off A. **Rnd 4** Join D in first sc of any corner, ch 3 (counts as 1 dc), dc, (ch 4, sl st in first ch from hook)—picot made, 2 dc in same space, (2 dc, picot, 2 dc) in next corner sc—group made; counting the ch-1's in rnd 3 as a st, work a group in every 3rd st and work corners with a group in each sc of corner as above, adjusting sts as needed, end sk 2 sts, join with sl st to beg ch. Fasten off.

materials

Chunky*USA by Lion Brand Yarn Co., 4oz/113g skeins, each approx 155yd/142m (acrylic)
4 skeins in #099 fisherman (C)
3 skeins in #100 snowcap white (D)
2 skeins each in #110 denim (A) and #152 skyscraper grey (B)

Size P/15 (10mm) crochet hook
OR SIZE TO OBTAIN GAUGE

prairie stripes

finished measurements

42" × 62"/106.5 × 157.5cm (not including border)

gauge

10 sts and 10 rows to 4"/10cm, over sc using size K/10½ (6.5mm) crochet hook.
TAKE TIME TO CHECK YOUR GAUGE.

notes

1 Afghan is made of three 14" × 62"/35.5 × 157.5cm panels.
2 To change colors when working panels, draw new color through 2 lps on hook to complete last sc, then ch and turn.
3 To change colors when working border, draw new color through lp on hook to complete sl st.

right panel

With A, ch 36. **Row 1** Sc in 2nd ch from hook and in each ch across—35 sts. Ch 1, turn. **Row 2** Sc in each sc across. Ch 1, turn. Rep row 2 for pat st and work in stripe pat as foll: *[6 rows A, 2 rows B] 4 times, [4 rows C, 4 rows A] 3 times, [2 rows D, 2 rows C, 2 rows A, 2 rows C] twice, 2 rows D; rep from * once more, end [6 rows A, 2 rows B] 3 times, 6 rows A—180 rows completed from beg; piece should measure 62"/157.5cm from beg. Fasten off.

center panel

With D, ch 36. Work rows 1 and 2 same as for right panel—35 sts. Ch 1, turn. Cont in sc and work in stripe pat as foll: [2 rows D, 2 rows C, 2 rows A, 2 rows C] twice, 2 rows A, [6 rows B, 2 rows A] twice, 6 rows B, [4 rows A, 2 rows C] 4 times, [4 rows D, 4 rows B, 2 rows C] 4 times, 4 rows D, 4 rows B, [4 rows A, 2 rows C] 4 times, 2 rows D, [6 rows B, 2 rows A] twice, 6 rows B, [2 rows D, 2 rows C, 2 rows A, 2 rows C] twice, end 2 rows D—180 rows completed from beg. Fasten off.

left panel

With A, ch 36. Work rows 1 and 2 same as for right panel—35 sts. Ch 1, turn. Cont in sc and work in stripe pat as foll: *[6 rows A, 2 rows B] 3 times, 6 rows A, [2 rows D, 2 rows C, 2 rows A, 2 rows C] twice, 2 rows D, [4 rows A, 4 rows C] 3 times, 2 rows B; rep from * once more, end [6 rows A, 2 rows B] 3 times, 6 rows A—180 rows completed from beg. Fasten off.

finishing

Sew panels tog invisibly.
Border
From RS, join C with a sl st in top right corner **Rnd 1** Ch 1, work 97 sc evenly spaced across top edge, work 3 sc in left top corner, work 138 sc evenly spaced along left side edge, work 3 sc in left bottom corner, work 97 sc evenly spaced along bottom edge, work 3 sc in right bottom corner, work 138 sc evenly spaced along right

(continued on page 135)

materials

Homespun by Lion Brand Yarn Co., 6oz/170g skeins, each approx 185yd/170m (acrylic/polyester)
4 skeins in #335 prairie (A)
3 skeins each in #334 gothic (B) and #327 plantation (C)
2 skeins in #307 antique

Size K/10 1/2 (6.5mm) crochet hook OR SIZE TO OBTAIN GAUGE

home essentials

A crocheted afghan lends a cozy touch to any living space.

ocean waves

intermediate

finished measurements

54" x 62½"/137 x 158cm

gauge

14½ sts and 6½ rows to 4"/10cm over pat st using size J/10 (6mm) crochet hook.
TAKE TIME TO CHECK YOUR GAUGE.

notes

1 Ch 3 counts as first dc in the next row.
2 Change color before ch-3 of last row.
3 To change color, work to last 2 lps on hook. Draw lp in next color through 2 lps on hook to complete st and proceed in next color.

afghan

With MC, ch 202.
Row 1 Dc in 4th ch from hook, 1 dc in each of next 2 ch, 3 dc in next ch, 1 dc in each of next 3 ch, *sk next 4 ch, work (1 dc, [ch 1, 1 dc] 4 times) all in next ch—open shell made, sk next 4 ch, 1 dc in each of next 3 ch, 3 dc in next ch, 1 dc in each of next 3 ch; rep from * across—200 sts. Ch 3, turn.
Row 2 Sk first dc, 1 dc in each of next 3 dc, 3 dc in next dc, 1 dc in each of next 3 dc, *sk next 2 dc, 1 sc in next ch-1 sp, [ch 3, 1 sc in next ch-1 sp] 3 times, sk next 2 dc, 1 dc in each of next 3 dc, 3 dc in next dc, 1 dc in each of next 3 dc; rep from * to last dc and turning ch (do not work into these sts). Ch 3, turn.
Row 3 Sk first dc, 1 dc in each of next 3 dc, 3 dc in next dc, 1 dc in each of next 3 dc, *sk next 2 dc and ch-3 sp, 1 open shell in next ch-3 sp, sk next ch-3 sp and 2 dc, 1 dc in each of next 3 dc, 3 dc in next dc, 1 dc in each of next 3 dc; rep from * to last dc and turning ch (do not work into these sts). Ch 3, turn.
Rep rows 2 and 3 twice more. ****Change to A and rep rows 2 and 3 once. Change to B and rep rows 2 and 3 twice. Change to A and rep rows 2 and 3 once. Change to MC and rep rows 2 and 3 3 times; rep from ** until piece measures approx 62"/158cm from beg, end with row 3 in MC.
Last row With MC, sk first dc, 1 dc in each of next 3 dc, 3 dc in next dc, 1 dc in each of next 3 dc, *sk next 2 dc, 1 sc in next ch-1 sp, [1 sc in next dc, 1 sc in next ch-1 sp] 3 times, sk next 2 dc, 1 dc in each of next 3 dc, 3 dc in next dc, 1 dc in each of next 3 dc; rep from * to last dc and turning ch (do not work into these sts). Fasten off.

finishing

Fringe

Cut 3 10"/25cm long strands of MC. Holding 3 strands tog, knot fringe evenly spaced across top and bottom edges.

materials

Super Value by Bernat®, 8oz/225g balls, each approx 445yd/406m (acrylic)
3 balls in #7704 medium navy (MC)
2 balls each in #7698 light navy (A) and #7681 pale navy (B)

Size J/10 (6mm) crochet hook
OR SIZE TO OBTAIN GAUGE

soft pastel diamonds

easy

finished measurements

50" x 70"/127 x 178cm

gauge

12 sts to 4"/10cm over pat st using size H/8 (5mm) crochet hook.
TAKE TIME TO CHECK YOUR GAUGE.

color pattern

Work 20 rows MC, 5 rows CC, 19 rows MC, 9 rows CC, 19 rows MC, 5 rows CC and 20 rows MC. These 97 rows form color pat.

afghan

With MC, ch 214.

Row 1 Dc in 4th ch from hook, dc in next 6 chs, *ch 2, sk 2 chs, dc in next 7 chs; rep from * across to last 6 chs, end ch 2, sk 2 chs, dc in last 4 chs. Ch 3, turn.

Row 2 Dc in next 2 dc, *ch 2, dc in ch-2 sp, ch 2, sk 1 dc, dc in next 5 dc; rep from * across, end ch 2, dc in last dc. Ch 3, turn.

Row 3 Dc in ch-2 sp, *ch 2, sk 1 dc, dc in next 3 dc, ch 2, dc in ch-2 sp, dc in dc, dc in ch-2 sp; rep from * across, end ch 2, sk 1 dc, dc in last 2 dc. Ch 5, turn.

Row 4 *Dc in ch-2 sp, dc in next 3 dc, dc in ch-2 sp, ch 2, sk 1 dc, dc in next dc, ch 2; rep from * across, end dc in ch-2 sp, and last 2 dc. Ch 3, turn.

Row 5 Dc in next 2 dc and ch-2 sp, *ch 2, dc in next ch-2 sp, dc in next 5 dc, dc in ch-2 sp *; rep from * across, end dc in top of turning ch. Ch 5, turn.

Row 6 *Sk 1 dc, dc in next 5 dc, ch 2, dc in ch-2 sp, ch 2; rep from * across, end sk 1 dc, dc in last 3 dc. Ch 3, turn.

Row 7 Dc in next dc, *ch 2, dc in ch-2 sp, dc in dc, dc in ch-2 sp, ch 2, sk 1 dc, dc in next 3 dc; rep from * across, end ch 2, dc in ch-2 sp and in top of turning ch. Ch 3, turn.

Row 8 Dc in next dc, *dc in ch-2 sp, ch 2, sk 1 dc, dc in next dc, ch 2, dc in ch-2 sp, dc in next 3 dc; rep from * across, end dc in ch-2 sp, ch 2, dc in last dc. Ch 3, turn.

Row 9 Dc in ch-2 sp, *dc in next 5 dc, dc in ch-2 sp, ch 2, dc in next ch-2 sp; rep from * across, end dc in last 3 dc. Ch 3, turn. Working in color pat, rep rows 2-9 for pat st until 97 rows have been completed. Fasten off.

finishing

Edging

Rnd 1 Join CC in any corner, work 3 sc in this and every corner; sc in each st across top and bottom. Work 2 sc across both sides in ch 3 and first dc of each row, end sl st to first sc. Ch 3, turn.

Rnd 2 Work 4 dc in first sc, *sk 2 sc, sc in next sc, sk 2 sc, work 5 dc in next sc; rep from * around, end sl st in 3rd ch of ch-3. Fasten off.

materials

Simply Soft® by Caron®, 3oz/85g skeins, each approx 163yd/150m (acrylic)
12 skeins in #2602 off white (MC)
5 skeins in #2705 soft green (CC)

Size H/8 (5mm) crochet hook
OR SIZE TO OBTAIN GAUGE

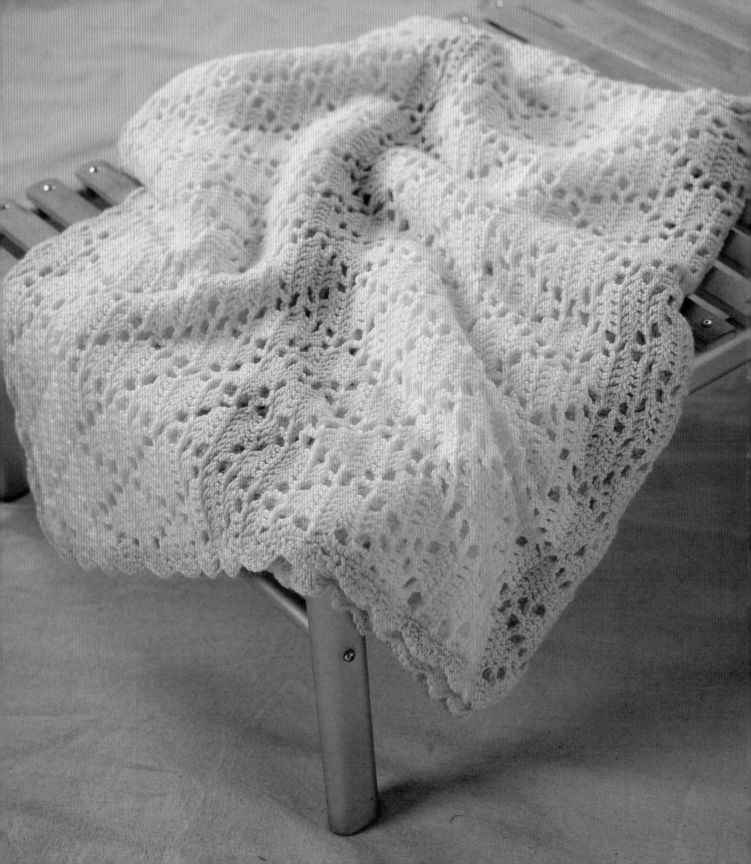

plaid tapestry

intermediate

finished measurements
50" x 64"/127 x 162.5cm

gauge
13 sts and 14 rows to 4"/10cm over sc using larger hook.
TAKE TIME TO CHECK YOUR GAUGE.

notes
1 Afghan is made of 6 ½"/16.5cm wide strips.
2 The strips are worked in sc using bobbins.
3 Wind colors A, B and C onto separate bobbins.

strip
(make 7)
With larger hook and A, ch 23.
Row 1 (RS) Sc in 2nd ch from hook and in next 5 ch, with B, sc in next 10 ch, with A, sc in last 6 ch—22 sts. Ch 1, turn.
Rows 2-4 Keeping to colors as established, sc across. Ch 1, turn.

Row 5 (RS) With D, sc across. Drop D. Go back to beg of row. Beg with A and rep rows 1 and 2. Drop Color A.
Row 8 Go back to beg of row (RS), pick up D and sc across. Drop D, pick up A.
Rows 9 and 10 Rep rows 1 and 2.
Rows 11-20 Work 6 sts using A, 10 sts using C and 6 sts using A. Work even for 10 rows. Rep rows 1-20 10 times, then rows 1-10 once. Fasten off.

finishing
Joining
From RS using smaller hook and D, work from bottom to top as foll: work a sl st ch between 2nd and 3rd st from each edge. Rep on all strips. Join strips from WS matching pat stripes
Edging
From RS with A and larger hook, join with 1 sl st at any point, ch 1, *sc in each sc and in each row; rep from * around, working 3 sc in each corner. Join rnd with sl st to beg ch. Ch 1, turn. Rep this rnd twice. **Last rnd** Working from left to right, sc in each st around. Join with a sl st in first sc. Fasten off.

materials
Wintuk® by Caron®, 3.5oz/6g skeins, each 150yd/137m (acrylic)
8 skeins in #3031 navy (A)
4 skeins each in #3032 rosewine (B), #3018 woodsy green (C) and #3021 oatmeal (D)

———————

Size H/8 and J/10 (5 and 6mm) crochet hooks OR SIZE TO OBTAIN GAUGE

———————

Bobbins

double diamond throw

experienced

finished measurements
48" x 63"/122 x 160cm

gauge
16 sts and 16 rows to 4"/10cm over sc using larger hook.
TAKE TIME TO CHECK YOUR GAUGE.

stitch glossary
FPtr (front post treble)
Yo twice, insert hook from front to back to front around post of stitch indicated, yo and pull up a lp even with last st worked and complete st.
Psc (picot sc)
Insert hook in next st, pull up a lp, [yo, draw through 1 lp on hook] 3 times, yo and draw through both lps on hook.

afghan
With larger hook, ch 166.
Row 1 (WS) Sc in 2nd ch from hook and in each ch across—165 sc. Ch 1, turn.
Row 2 Work 13 sc, mark last sc for center st, sc in next 48 sts, mark last st, sc in next 44, mark last st, sc in 48, mark last st, sc in last 12. Ch 1, turn.
Row 3 and all WS rows Sc in each st across. Ch 1, turn.
Row 4 Sc in first sc, (*FPtr around next st 3 rows below, sk 1, sc in next st, FPtr around next st 3 rows below, sk 1*, sc in next 7, **work dc around post of marked st in 2 rows below, sk 1, sc in next sc, work 1 dc around same marked st, sk 1, **sc

in next 7 sc*; rep between *'s) sc in 35; rep between **'s, sc in next 41; rep between **'s, sc in 35; rep between ( )'s, sc. Ch 1, turn.
Row 6 Sc in first st, (*FPtr around FPtr, sk 1, sc in next st, FPtr around FPtr, sk 1*, sc in next 6, **dc around post of dc, sk 1, sc in next 3, dc around dc, sk 1, **sc in next 6, rep between *'s), sc in next 34 sts, dc around dc, sk 1, sc in next 3, dc around dc, sk 1, sc in next 39; rep between **'s, sc in 34; rep between ( )'s, sc. Ch 1, turn.
Row 8 Sc in first st, (*FPtr around FPtr, sk 1, sc, FPtr around FPtr, sk 1*, sc in next 5, **dc, sk 1, sc in next 5, dc, sk 1, **sc in next 5; rep between *'s) sc in next 33, dc, sk 1, sc in next 5, dc, sk 1, sc in next 37; rep between **'s, sc in next 33; rep between ( )'s. Ch 1, turn.
Row 10 Sc in first st, (*tr, sk 1, sc, tr, sk 1, *sc in next 4, **dc, sk 1, sc in next 7, dc, sk 1**, sc in next 4; rep between *'s), sc in next 14, Psc , [sc in next 17, rep between **'s, sc in next 17, Psc] twice, sc in next 14, rep between *'s, sc in next 4; rep between **'s, sc in next 4; rep between *'s, sc in last st, ch 1, turn.
Row 12 Sc in first st, *tr, sk 1, sc , tr, sk 1, *sc in next 3, **dc, sk 1, sc in next 9, dc, sk 1**, sc in next 3; rep between *'s, sc in next 13, Psc, sc, Psc, work [sc next 15, rep between **'s, sc in next 15, Psc, sc, Psc] twice, work 13 sc; rep between *'s, sc in next 3; rep between **'s, sc in next 3; rep between *'s, sc in last st. Ch 1, turn.
Row 14 Sc in first st, *tr, sk 1, sc, tr, sk 1, *sc in next 2, dc, sk 1, sc in next 6, mark last sc for center st, sc in next 5, dc, sk 1**, sc in next 2, rep between *'s, sc in next 12, Psc, [sc, Psc] twice, work [sc in 13, rep between **'s, sc in 13, (Psc,

(continued on page135)

materials
Simply Soft® by Caron®, 3oz/85g skeins, each approx 163yd/150m (acrylic) 24 skeins in color of your choice

Size H/8 and I/9 (5 and 5.5mm) crochet hooks OR SIZE TO OBTAIN GAUGE

Open ended stitch markers

bouclé blue

finished measurements

49" x 53"/124 x 134.5cm

gauge

16 sts and 20 rows to 4"/10cm over pat st using size 10 (6mm) needles.
TAKE TIME TO CHECK YOUR GAUGE.

stitch glossary

Tw2B
K into 2nd st on needle, then into 1st st on needle, slipping both sts off tog.
Tw2BP
P into 2nd st on needle, then into 1st st on needle, slipping both sts off tog.

pattern stitch

Row 1 (WS) Purl.
Row 2 P1, *Tw2B, p1; rep from * to end.
Row 3 K1, *Tw2BP, k1; rep from * to end.
Row 4 Knit.
Rep rows 1-4 for pat st.

afghan

Cast on 136 sts.
**Purl 3 rows (mark first row as WS).
Row 4 (RS) K1, *yo, SKP; rep from *, end k1.**
Rep last 4 rows 3 times more.
Next row Purl.
Next row P4, *M1, p3; rep from * to end—169 sts. Cont in pat st and work even until piece measures 49½"/125.5cm from beg, end with a RS row.
Next row (WS) K4, *k2tog, k3; rep from * to end—136 sts.
Next row K1, *yo, SKP; rep from *, end k1.
Rep from ** to ** same as above 4 times. Purl next 2 rows. Bind off all sts purlwise.
Side edging
From RS, pick up and knit 173 sts evenly spaced along side edge. Knit next row.
Next row K1, *yo, SKP; rep from *, end k1.
Rep from ** to ** same as above 4 times. Purl next 2 rows. Bind off all sts purlwise. Rep along opposite side edge.

materials

*Softee Chunky by Bernat®, 3 ½oz/100g balls, each approx 164yd/150m (acrylic)
11 balls #40119 Denim*

Size 10 (6mm) circular needle, 29"/73.5cm long OR SIZE TO OBTAIN GAUGE

alaskan nights

intermediate

finished measurements

42" x 66"/106.5 x 167.5cm

gauge

10 sts and 8 rows to 4"/10cm over sc using size N/15 (10mm) crochet hook and 2 strands of yarn held tog.
TAKE TIME TO CHECK YOUR GAUGE.

note

Use 2 strands of yarn held tog throughout.

afghan

With two strands yarn held tog, ch 152.

Row 1 Sc in 2nd ch from hook and in each ch across—151 sts. Turn.

Rows 2-5 Ch 1, sc in each sc across; turn. End of row 5, do not turn.

Row 6 Working from left to right, work reverse sc in front lp of each sc across, ch 1, do not turn.

Row 7 Working from right to left, sc in the back lp of each sc not worked in previous row, ch 1, turn.

Row 8 Sc in each sc across, ch 1, turn.

Row 9 (RS) Note Each cable is completed before the next cable is begun, you will reverse direction twice to complete each separate cable. Work as folls: *Sc in first st, make cable as follows: ch 3, sk 2 sts, sc in next st, turn, sc in each of the 3 chs, sl st in the sc before ch was begun, turn (cable made), holding the cable towards you, work 1 sc in each of the 2 sk sts below the cable, ch 3, sk the sc where the previous ch is attached and the next 2 sts, sc in next st, turn, sc in each of the 3 chs, sl st in the sc before ch was begun, turn; holding the cable towards you, sc in 2 sk sts as before*; rep from * to * across, ending by working sc in last st (same sc used to attach last ch-3), ch 1 turn.

Row 10 Sc in first sc, sc in each of next 2 sc behind first cable, *work 2 sc in first sc behind next cable, sc in next sc behind same cable*; rep from * to * across, ending by working sc in first sc of prev row, ch 1, turn.

Row 11 Sc in each sc across, do not turn.

Row 12 Rep row 6.

Row 13 Rep row 7.

Rows 14-20 Sc in each sc across, ch 1, turn.

Row 21 (RS) Sl st in first sc, ch 3, in row 18, work a sl st around post of 4th sc as follows: insert hook at right of post from front to back and again to front at left of st, hook yarn and draw lp through and complete st as a sl st, ch 3, in row 20, sk 5 sc, sl st in next sc, *ch 3, in row 18, sk 5 sc, sl st around post of next sc, ch 3: in row 20, sk 5 sc, sl st in next sc*; rep from * to * across, (Do not turn, you will now be working from left to right across row just worked.) **ch 7, sk 5 sc as before, sl st in same sc where ch-3 was attached, working sl st over prev sl st**; rep from ** to ** across ending last rep by working a sl st in last sc of row 20 (same st where first sl st of row 21 was worked), ch 2, do not turn.

Row 22 (RS) *Sk st used to anchor ch-7, sc in each of next 5 sc sk in row 21, ch 1*; rep from * to * across keeping each ch-7 to RS of work, ending last rep by working sc in each of last 5 sc sk in row 21, sc in same sc used to attach last ch-3 in row 21, ch 1, turn.

(continued on page 136)

materials

Red Heart Super Saver by Coats & Clark™, 6oz/170g skeins, each approx 348yd/319m (acrylic)
14 skeins in #4313 aran fleck

Size N/15 (10mm) crochet hook
OR SIZE TO OBTAIN GAUGE

floral water lily

experienced

finished measurements

42" x 58"/106.5 x 147.5cm

gauge

16 sts and 14 rows to 4"/10cm over basic afghan st using size J/10 (6mm) afghan hook.
TAKE TIME TO CHECK YOUR GAUGE.

panel

(make 4)

With afghan hook and A, ch 27. Work in basic afghan st as foll:

Row 1 (first half row) Insert hook into 2nd ch from hook, (working from right to left) yo, draw yarn through st, (insert hook in next ch, yo, draw through st) across—27 lps on hook.

Row 1 (second half row) Yo, draw yarn through one lp on hook, *yo, draw yarn through 2 lps on hook**; rep from * to ** across (working backwards from left to right). **Note** One loop rem on hook and counts as first lp of next row. Rep row 1 foll chart until there are 170 rows.

Row 171 Sl st in each vertical st (or "bar") across—27 sts each row. Fasten off.

finishing

Panel border

With RS of panel facing and crochet hook, join C in top right corner st. **Rnd 1** Ch 1, sc in same st as joining, sc in next 2 sts, *[sk next st, sc in next 3 sts] 5 times, sk next st, sc in next 2 sts, ch 2, sc in each row end st on length of panel to next corner, ch 2**, sc in each 3 sts; rep from * to ** around. Join with a sl st in beg sc. Fasten off. **Rnd 2** Join B in 2nd sc to the left of top right corner, ch 3 (counts as 1 dc), dc in sc to the right of dc just made, *sk next sc, dc in next sc, dc in sc to the right of dc just made**; rep from * to ** around, working (2 dc, ch 2, 2 dc) in each corner ch-2 sp. Join with a sl st in 3rd ch of ch-3. Fasten off. **Rnd 3** Join A in top right corner ch-2 sp, ch 3 (counts 1 dc), (dc, ch 2, 2 dc) in same corner ch-2 sp, work 2 dc in between each set of 2 dc groups around, working (2 dc, ch 2, 2 dc) in each corner ch-2 sp. Join with a sl st in 3rd ch of ch-3. Fasten off.

Embroidery

Following chart, cross-stitch design on each panel.

Panel assembly

With tops of 2 panels aligned with RS tog and crochet hook, join A in corner ch-2 sps, ch 1, working through both thicknesses sl st in each st across to next corner ch-2 sp. Fasten off.

Afghan border

With RS facing and crochet hook, join A in upper right corner dc. **Rnd 1** Ch 3 (counts as 1 dc), dc evenly spaced around, working (2 dc, ch 2, 2 dc) in each corner. **Rnd 2** Join B in 2nd dc to the left of upper right corner, ch 3 (counts as 1 dc), dc in dc to the right of dc just made, *sk next dc, dc in next dc, dc in sk dc to the right of dc just made**; rep from * to ** around, working (2 dc, ch 2, 2 dc) in each corner ch-2 sp. Join with a sl st in 3rd ch of ch-3. Fasten off.

materials

TLC Essentials by Coats & Clark™, 6oz/170g skeins, each approx 326yd/299m (acrylic)
6 skeins in #2313 aran (A)
1 skein each in #2772 lt country rose (C), #2673 med thyme (D) and #2531 lt plum (E)

TLC Essentials by Coats & Clark™ 4½oz/128g skeins, each approx 255yd/234m (acrylic)
3 skeins in #2966 waterlily (B)

Size J/10 (6mm) afghan hook
OR SIZE TO OBTAIN GAUGE

Size J/10 (6mm) crochet hook

Tapestry needle

(see chart on page 136)

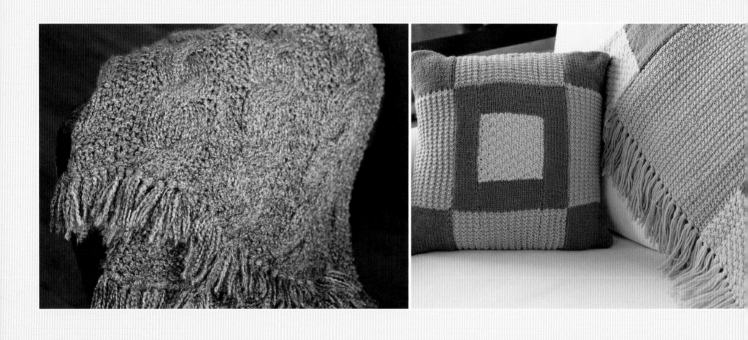

timeless classics

Hand-knit afghans make priceless family heirlooms that can be passed on from generation to generation.

open windows set

easy

finished measurements

Afghan
55" x 68"/139.5 x 173cm
Pillow
16" x 16"/40.5 x 40.5cm

gauge

20 sts and 26 rows to 4"/10cm over St st using size 7 (4.5mm) needles.
TAKE TIME TO CHECK YOUR GAUGE.

pattern 1

(worked over 56 sts)
Row 1 (RS) With MC, knit.
Row 2 K1, p54, k1.
Rep rows 1 and 2 for pat 1.

pattern 2

(multiple of 4 sts)
Rows 1 and 2 With A, *k2, p2; rep from * to end.
Rows 3 and 4 *P2, k2; rep from * to end.
Rep rows 1-4 for pat 2.

pattern 3

(multiple of 2 sts)
Row 1 (WS) With B, *k1, p1; rep from * to end.
Row 2 Purl.
Rep rows 1 and 2 for pat 3.

afghan

Panel 1
(make 3)
With straight needles and MC, cast on 56 sts. Work in pat 1 for 13"/33cm, end with row 2.
Next row (RS) With A, knit. Work in pat 2 for 4"/10cm, end with row 2 or 4.
Next row (RS) With B, knit. Work in pat 3 for 13"/33cm, end with row 1. Work in pat 1 for 4"/10cm, end with row 2.
Next row (RS) With A, knit. Work in pat 2 for 13"/33cm, end with row 2 or 4.
Next row (RS) With B, knit. Work in pat 3 for 4"/10cm, end with row 1. Work in pat 1 for 13"/33cm, end with row 2.
Next row (RS) With A, knit. Work in pat 2 for 4"/10cm, end with pat row 2 or 4. Bind off.

Panel 2
(make 2)
With straight needles and A, cast on 56 sts.
Next row (RS) Knit. Work in pat 2 for 4"/10cm, end with row 2 or 4.
Next row (RS) With B, knit. Work in pat 3 for 13"/33cm, end with row 1. Work in pat 1 for 4"/10cm, end with row 2.
Next row (RS) With A, knit. Work in pat 2 for 13"/33cm, end with row 2 or 4.
Next row (RS) With B, knit. Work in pat 3 for 4"/10cm, end with row 1. Work in pat 1 for 13"/33cm, end with row 2.
Next row (RS) With A, knit. Work in pat 2 for 4"/10cm, end with row 2 or 4.
Next row (RS) With B, knit. Work in pat 3 for 13"/33cm, end with row 1. Bind off.

(continued on page 137)

materials

Decor by Patons®, 3½oz/100g balls, each approx 210yd/192m (acrylic/wool)

Afghan
8 balls each in #1636 sage green (MC) and #1630 pale taupe (A)
7 balls in #1635 pale sage green (B)

Pillow
2 balls in #1635 pale sage green (B)
1 ball each in #1636 sage green (MC) and #1630 pale taupe (A)

One pair size 7 (4.5mm) needles
OR SIZE TO OBTAIN GAUGE

Size 7 (4.5mm) circular needle 36"/90cm
16"/40.5cm pillow form

lacy fern afghan

intermediate

finished measurements

52" x 64"/132 x 162.5cm

gauge

33 sts and 24 rows to 7"/17.5cm over pat st using size 10 (6mm) needle.
TAKE TIME TO CHECK YOUR GAUGE.

center panel

Cast on 166 sts. Work back and forth as foll:
Foundation row (WS) Purl.
Row 1 *K1, p1, SK2P, k10, yo, k1, yo, p2, yo, k1, yo, k10, k3tog, p1; rep from * 4 times, end k1.
Row 2 and all WS rows Purl the p sts and knit the k sts as they face you.
Row 3 *K1, p1, SK2P, k9, yo, k1, yo, k1, p2, k1, yo, k1, yo, k9, p1; rep from * 4 times, end k1.
Row 5 *K1, p1, SK2P, k8, yo, k1, yo, k2, k2, yo, k1, yo, k8, p1; rep from * 4 times, end k1.
Row 7 *K1, p1, SK2P, k7, yo, k1, yo, k3, p2, k3, yo, k1, yo, k7, p1; rep from * 4 times, end k1.
Row 9 *K1, p1, SK2P, k6, yo, k1, yo, k4, p2, k4, yo, k1, yo, k6, p1; rep from * 4 times, end k1.
Row 11 *K1, p1, SK2P, k5, yo, k1, yo, k5, p2, k5, yo, k1, yo, k5, p1; rep from * 4 times, end k1.
Row 12 Rep row 2.
Rep rows 1-12 for pat st 17 more times. Bind off.

left panel

Cast on 36 sts. Work back and forth as foll:
Foundation row (WS) Purl.
Row 1 K3, p2, [SKP, k2, yo, k2] twice, k1, place marker, p2, yo, k1, yo, k10, k3tog, p1, k1.
Row 2 and all even rows P1, k1, p14, k2, p13, k5.
Row 3 K3, p2, [SKP, k2, yo, k2] twice, k1, sl marker, p2, k1, yo, k1, yo, k9, k3tog, p1, k1.
Row 5 K3, p2, [SKP, k2, yo, k2] twice, k1, sl marker, p2, k2, yo, k1, yo, k8, k3tog, p1, k1.
Row 7 K3, p2, k3, *yo, k2, k2tog**, k2; rep from * to **, sl marker, p2, k3, yo, k1, yo, k7, k3tog, p1, k1.
Row 9 K3, p2, k3, *yo, k2, k2tog**, k2; rep from * to **, sl marker, p2, k4, yo, k1, yo, k6, k3tog, pl, k1.
Row 11 K3, p2, k3, *yo, k2, k2tog**, k2; rep from * to **, sl marker, p2, k5, yo, k1, yo, k5, k3tog, p1, k1.
Row 12 Rep row 2.
Rep rows 1-12 for pat st 17 more times. Bind off.

right panel

Cast on 36 sts. Work back and forth as foll:
Foundation row (WS) Purl.
Row 1 K1, p1, SK2P, k10, yo, k1, yo, p2, place marker, [SKP, k2, yo, k2] twice, k1, p2, k3.
Row 2 and all WS rows K5, p13, k2, p14, k1, p1.
Row 3 K1, p1, SK2P, k9, yo, k1, yo, k1, p2, [SKP, k2, yo, k2] twice, k1, p2, k3.
Row 5 K1, p1, SK2P, k8, yo, k1, yo, k2, p2, [SKP, k2, yo, k2] twice, k1, p2, k3.
Row 7 K1, p1, SK2P, k7, yo, k1, yo, k3, p2, k3, *yo, k2, k2tog**, k2; rep from * to **, p2, k3.
Row 9 K1, p1, SK2P, k6, yo, k1, yo, k4, p2, k3, *yo, k2, k2tog**, k2; rep from * to **, p2, k3.
Row 11 K1, p1, SK2P, k5, yo, k1, yo, k5, p2, k3, *yo, k2, k2tog**, k2; rep from * to **, p2, k3.
Row 12 Rep row 2.
Rep rows 1-12 for pat st 17 more times. Bind off.

(continued on page 137)

materials

Red Heart Super Saver by Coats & Clark™, 8oz/226g skeins, each approx 452yd/414m (acrylic)
6 skeins in #631 lt sage

Size 10 (6mm) circular needle, 36"/91.5cm long OR
SIZE TO OBTAIN GAUGE

Size G/6 (4mm) crochet hook

Stitch markers

handloomed homespun

easy

finished measurements
44" x 56"/111.5 x 142cm

gauge
12 sts and 20 rows to 4"/10cm over reverse St st using size 10 (6mm) needles.
TAKE TIME TO CHECK YOUR GAUGE.

pattern stitch
Row 1 (WS) Knit.
Row 2 (RS) K2, p across to last 2 sts, k2.
Rep rows 1 and 2 for pat st.

notes
1 Afghan is worked in strips. Strips are joined, then edging is worked on top, bottom and side edges.
2 If desired, you can work the rectangles, that are made in each color making up the strips, as separate pieces. Arrange them as desired and seam them to make strips. Then finish as Strip Version.

strip version
Make 6 per color or with colors arranged as desired.
Strip 1
With straight needles and A, cast on 18 sts. *Work 5 rows in garter st (k every row). Beg with a WS row, work in pat st for 7"/17.5cm, end with a RS row. Work 5 rows in garter st*. Cont to follow chart for Strip 1, change to B (on RS row); rep from * to * above. Cont to follow chart

for Strip 1; rep from * to * until all 6 colors from Strip 1 have been completed. Bind off 18 sts.
Strip 2
Work as for Strip 1, follow chart for Strip 2 colors.
Strip 3
Work as for Strip 1, follow chart for Strip 3 colors.
Strip 4
Work as for Strip 1, follow chart for Strip 4 colors.
Strip 5
Work as for Strip 1, follow chart for Strip 5 colors.
Strip 6
Work as for Strip 1, follow chart for Strip 6 colors.

finishing
Join strips tog using flat seam. Weave in ends.
Border pattern
Using circular needle and C, pick up and k 108 sts along top edge of afghan. Working back and forth with C, k 3 more rows, inc 1 st at each end of next RS row. Change to D. With D, k 6 rows, inc 1 st at each end of every RS row. Change to B; do not cut color D (RS row). **Note There will be no incs in color B rows. **Next row** *Sl 2 sts as if to p wyib, k4 sts in B*; rep from * to * across, end with sl 2 sts. **Next row** *Sl 2 sts wyif, k4 sts in B*; rep from * to * across, end with sl 2 sts. With D and resuming incs on RS rows, work 2 rows knitting previous color D sts and sl color B sts keeping yarn across sl sts on WS. Return to color B and work 2 rows of sl st pat as above (no incs). Return to color D, k 8 rows inc 1 st at each end of RS row. Bind off all sts on last row.** Rep border pat from ** to ** on bottom edge of afghan. Rep border pat from ** to ** on each

(continued on page 137)

materials
Homespun by Lion Brand Yarn Co., 6oz/170g skeins, each approx 185yd/170m (acrylic/polyester)
1 skein each in #307 antique (A) and #301 shaker (E)
2 skeins each in #312 edwardian (B), #311 rococo (C) and #318 sierra (D)

One pair size 10 (6mm) needles
OR SIZE TO OBTAIN GAUGE

Size 10 (6mm) circular needle, 32"/80cm long

first cable afghan

easy

finished measurements

40" x 54"/101.5 x 137cm (without fringe)

gauge

8 sts and 12 rows to 4"/10cm over St st using size 15 (10mm) needle and 2 strands of yarn held tog.
TAKE TIME TO CHECK YOUR GAUGE.

notes

1 Use 2 strands of yarn held tog throughout.
2 Afghan is knit in 3 panels.

seed stitch

(multiple of 2 sts plus 1)
Row 1 *K1, p1; repeat from *, end k1.
Rep row 1 for seed st.

cable pattern

(worked over 8 sts)
Rows 1, 3, 7, 9 and 11 (RS) K 8.
Rows 2, 4, 6, 8, 10 and 12 P 8.
Row 5 Sl 4 sts to cn and hold to *back*, k4, k4 from cn.
Rep rows 1-12 for cable pat.

panel

(make 3)
With 2 strands of yarn held tog, cast on 27 sts.
Beg pats
Row 1 (RS) Work 3 sts in seed st, 8 sts in cable pat, 5 sts in seed st, 8 sts in cable pat and 3 sts in seed st. Beg with row 2, work even in pat sts as established until panel measures 54"/137cm from beg, end with row 4 of cable pat. Bind off loosely in pat sts.

finishing

Sew panels tog. Weave in ends.
Fringe
For each fringe, cut 5 strands 8"/20.5cm long. Use hook to pull through and knot fringe. Attach fringe close tog (approx 60 fringe sets per side).

materials

Homespun by Lion Brand Yarn Co., 6oz/170g skeins, each approx 185yd/170m (acrylic/polyester) 8 skeins in #346 bella vista

Size 15 (10mm) circular knitting needle, 29"/73.5cm long OR SIZE TO OBTAIN GAUGE

Cable needle (cn)

Size J/10 (6mm) crochet hook for fringe

rustic blocks

easy

finished measurements

44" x 64"/111.5 x 162.5cm (without border)

gauge

12 sts and 24 rows to 4"/10cm over garter st using size 11 (8mm) needles.
TAKE TIME TO CHECK YOUR GAUGE.

note

Afghan is worked in 11 vertical strips.

afghan

Referring to assembly chart and beg at lower right hand corner with A, cast on 12 sts. Work in garter st for 48 rows (24 ridges). Cont as per chart, change colors and work 24 rows of each color. Bind off when last color block on each strip is complete. Complete the 11 strips.

finishing

Sew strips tog invisibly.
Border
Each side is worked separately. With RS facing and C, pick up and k 123 sts evenly spaced along top edge of afghan. Working in garter st, inc 1 st each end every other row in color sequence as foll: 1 more row C, 2 rows K and 2 rows H. Bind off. Work bottom edge to correspond. Side edges are worked in the same manner, picking up 186 sts. Sew corners invisibly.

assembly chart

D	J	B	M	G	D	J	B	M	G	D
C	H	K	N	I	C	H	K	N	I	C
B	M	J	E	F	B	M	J	E	F	B
A	G	B	L	H	A	G	B	L	H	A
D	J	A	M	G	D	J	A	M	G	D
C	H	K	N	I	C	H	K	N	I	C
B	M	J	E	F	B	M	J	E	F	B
A	G	B	L	H	A	G	B	L	H	A

X begin here

BOTTOM

materials

Wool-Ease Chunky by Lion Brand Yarn Co.,
5oz/140g balls each approx
153yd/140m (acrylic/wool)
2 balls each in #180 evergreen (A),
#187 foliage (B), #152 charcoal (C),
#127 walnut (G), #141 appleton (H),
#109 royal (J) and #173 willow (M)
1 ball each in #147 boysenberry (D),
#139 huckleberry (E), #149 greystone (F),
#107 bluebell (I), #178 Nantucket (K),
#115 Bay Harbor (L) and
#145 Concord (N)

One pair size 11 (8 mm) knitting needles,
OR SIZE TO OBTAIN GAUGE

preppy ripple throw

easy

finished measurements

40" × 81"/101.5 × 205.5cm

gauge

18 sts to 7½"/19cm and 16 rows to 4¾"/12cm over ripple pat using size 13 (9mm) needles. TAKE TIME TO CHECK YOUR GAUGE.

note

Omit last 3 stripes if you would like a 62"/157.5cm length.

ripple pattern

(multiple of 18 sts plus 6)
Row 1 (RS) Knit.
Row 2 K3, p to last 3 sts, k3.
Row 3 K3, *[k2tog] 3 times, [yo, k1] 6 times, [k2tog] 3 times; rep from * to last 3 sts, k3.
Row 4 Rep row 2.
Rows 5-16 Rep rows 1-4
Rep rows 1-16 for ripple pat.

afghan

With A, cast on 96 sts. Work rows 1-16 of ripple pat in color sequence as foll: A, B, C, A, B, C, A, B, C, A, B, C and A. When 13 stripes are completed, bind off loosely.

materials

Wool-Ease Thick & Quick by Lion Brand Yarn Co., 6oz/170g balls, each approx 108yd/99m (acrylic/wool)
3 balls each in #110 navy (A), #098 fisherman (B) and #182 pine (C)

Size 13 (9 mm) knitting needles
OR SIZE TO OBTAIN GAUGE

octagon afghan

experienced

finished measurements

Afghan
48" x 60"/122 x 152.5cm
Full-sized Bedspread
81" x 81"/205.5 x 205.5cm

gauge

16 sts and 32 rows to 4"/10cm over garter st using size 8 (5mm) needle.
TAKE TIME TO CHECK YOUR GAUGE.

stitch glossary

l/r dec (left/right decrease)
On left needle, pull the second stitch over the first stitch, knit first stitch.

octagons

Make 20 (49). With MC and dpns, cast on 8 sts, dividing sts evenly on 4 dpns. Join and place marker at beg of rnd. **Note** Change to circular needle when there are too many sts for dpns.
Rnd 1 and all odd rnds Knit.
Rnd 2 *Yo, k1; rep from * 7 more times—16 sts.
Rnd 4 *Yo, k2; rep from * 7 more times—24 sts.
Rnd 6 *Yo, k3; rep from * 7 more times—32 sts.
Rnd 8 *Yo, k4; rep from * 7 more times—40 sts.
Rnd 10 *Yo, k5; rep from * 7 more times 48 sts.
Rnd 12 *Yo, k6; rep from * 7 more times—56 sts.
Rnd 14 *Yo, k7; rep from * 7 more times—64 sts.
Rnd 16 *Yo, k8; rep from * 7 more times—72 sts.
Rnd 18 *Yo, k1, yo, l/r dec, k6; rep from * 7 more times—80 sts.

Rnd 20 *Yo, k1, [yo, l/r dec] twice, k5; rep from * 7 more times—88 sts.
Rnd 22 *Yo, k1, [yo, l/r dec] 3 times, k4; rep from * 7 more times—96 sts.
Rnd 24 *Yo, k1, [yo, l/r dec] 4 times, k3; rep from * 7 more times—104 sts.
Rnd 26 *Yo, k1, [yo, l/r dec] 5 times, k2; rep from * 7 more times—112 sts.
Rnd 28 *Yo, k1, [yo, l/r dec] 6 times, k1; rep from * 7 more times—120 sts.
Rnd 30 *Yo, k1, [yo, l/r dec] 7 more times—128 sts.
Rnd 31 Knit. Bind off.

squares

Make 12 (36). With CC and circular needle, cast on 16 sts. **Note** Work back and forth on circular needle.
Row 1 and all odd rows Purl.
Row 2 K1, [yo, l/r dec] 7 times, end k1.
Row 4 K2, [yo, l/r dec] 7 times.
Rows 6, 10, 14 and 18 Rep row 2.
Rows 8, 12, 16, and 20 Rep row 4.
Row 21 Purl. Bind off.

finishing

Crochet or sew stars into strips of 5 (7) stars. Crochet or sew into 4 (7) strips of stars. Connect strips, placing squares to fill space between stars. Do not connect squares to outside edges of afghan/bedspread.
Border
Notes Work across 3 sides of each octagon across top and bottom edges. Work across 2 sides of first and last octagons and 3 sides of all

(continued on page 138)

materials

Wool-Ease by Lion Brand Yarn Co.,
3oz/85g balls, each approx
197yd/181m (acrylic/wool)
9 (18) balls in #099 fisherman (MC)
2 (4) balls in #152 oxford grey (CC)

Size 8 (5mm) circular needle, 29"/73.5cm
long OR SIZE TO OBTAIN GAUGE

One set (5) size 8 (5mm) dpn
Stitch markers in two colors

Large-eyed, blunt needle or crochet hook
for joining motifs

all natural cables

easy

finished measurements

45" x 61" (52" x 67")/114.5 x 155cm (132 x 170cm)

gauge

13 sts and 18 ¾ rows to 4"/10cm over seed st using size 11 (8mm) needles.
TAKE TIME TO CHECK YOUR GAUGE.

stitch glossary

M1 (make 1 st)
An increase worked by inserting left needle from back to front under horizontal strand between st just worked and next st on left needle. Purl this strand through front loop to twist it.

seed stitch

(over odd number of sts)
Row 1 *K1, p1; rep from *, end k1.
Rep row 1 for seed st.

cable

(worked over 12 sts)
Rows 1, 5, 7, and 9 (RS) P2, k8, p2.
Rows 2, 4, 6, 8 and 10 K2, p8, k2.
Row 3 P2, sl next 4 sts to cn and hold in *front*, k4, k4 from cn, p2.
Rep rows 1-10 for cable pat.

afghan

Cast on 117 (135) sts. Work in seed st for 15 rows.
Beg pat sts
Set up (inc) row (WS) *Seed st over 9 sts, k into front and back of next st, p3, M1, p4, k into front and back of next st; rep from *, end seed st over last 9 sts—135 (156) sts. Work pat sts as foll: *seed st over 9 sts, cable over 12 sts; rep from *, end seed st over last 9 sts. Cont working seed st as established and rep cable rows 1-10 until afghan measures approx 57 (64)"/144.5 (162.5)cm, ending with an even-numbered row.
Dec row *Seed st over 9 sts, p1, k1, p2tog, k1, p1, k2tog, p1, k1, p2tog; rep from *, end seed st over last 9 sts. Cont in seed st for 15 rows. Bind off.

materials

Wool-Ease Chunky by Lion Brand Yarn Co., 5oz/140g balls, each 153yd/140m (acrylic/wool)
10 (13) balls in # 402 wheat

Size 11 (8mm) circular needle, 36"/91.5cm long OR SIZE TO OBTAIN GAUGE

Cable needle (cn)

garden sprinkling can

experienced

finished measurements
48" x 64"/122 x 162.5cm

gauge
8 sts and 14 rows to 4"/10cm over basic afghan st using size H/8 (5mm) afghan hook.
TAKE TIME TO CHECK YOUR GAUGE.

note
Afghan is worked in basic afghan stitch with worked-in chart pattern and applied borders.

basic afghan stitch
Using afghan hook, ch number of sts indicated.
First half row Insert hook into 2nd ch from hook, (working from right to left) yo, draw yarn through st, *insert hook in next ch, yo, draw through st; rep from * across.
Second half row Yo, draw yarn through one lp on hook, *yo, draw yarn through 2 lps on hook; rep from * across (working backwards from left to right). **Note** One lp rem on hook and counts as first lp of next row.

charted panel
With afghan hook and MC, ch 110. Foll chart reading from right to left, and bottom to top. After row 103, turn chart upside down and work other half of afghan from right to left and bottom to top of inverted chart for another 103 rows. At end, sl st across in each bar to close—206 rows. Fasten off.

side panels
(make 2)
With afghan hook and MC, ch 23. Work in basic afghan stitch for 206 rows. At end, sl st across in each bar to close—206 rows. Fasten off.

finishing
Embroidery
Separate a length of F into 2 ply sections and back-stitch two antennae to top of each butterfly.
Border
Row 1 From RS with crochet hook, join MC with a sl st in corner of chart panel, sc in each row along side, sl st in last—206 sts. Turn. **Row 2 (WS)** Ch 1, sc in next sc; draw up a lp in next sc, [yo and through 1 lp] 3 times, yo through 2 lps on hook—bead st made. Keeping bead st in front of work, sc in next sc, *bead st in next sc, sc in next sc; rep from * to end—206 sts. Turn. **Row 3** Ch 3, *dc in next sc, dc behind bead st; rep from * to end—206 dc. Fasten off. **Row 4** Join A in first dc, sc in same st, *bead st in next dc, sc in next dc; rep from * to last st, sc in top of ch-3. Turn. **Row 5** Rep row 3. **Row 6** Join F and rep row 4. **Row 7** Join A and rep row 5. **Row 8** Ch 1, sc in each st across—206 sc. Turn. Fasten off. **Row 9** Join MC in first st, ch 3, *dc behind bead st, dc in next sc; rep from * to end. Turn. **Row 10** Rep row 8. Rep rows 1-10 on opposite side of chart panel.
Joining
Place side panel over chart panel with RS tog. Sl st through outer lps of each piece from top to bottom.

(continued on page 139)

materials
*Red Heart Super Saver by Coats & Clark™, 8oz/226g skeins, each approx 452yd/414m (acrylic)
5 skeins in #316 soft white (MC)
1 skein each in #372 rose pink (B), #374 country rose (C), #341 lt grey (D) #362 spruce (E) and #400 grey heather (F)*

*Red Heart Fiesta by Coats & Clark™, 6oz/170g skeins, each approx 330yd/302m (acrylic/nylon)
1 skein in #6341 millennium (A)*

*Size H/8 (5mm) flexible afghan hook
OR SIZE TO OBTAIN GAUGE*

Size H/8 (5mm) crochet hook

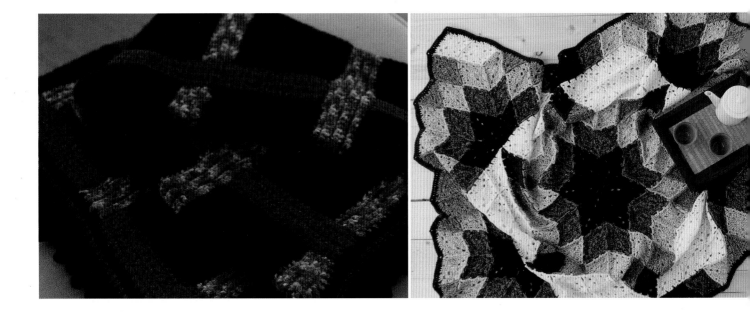

quilty pleasures

Crocheted quilts bring back fond memories of bygone days.

country blue

materials

*Simply Soft® Ombres by Caron®,
3oz/85g skeins, each approx
178yd/163m (acrylic)
9 skeins in #2720 country blue ombre (A)*

*Simply Soft® Solids by Caron®,
3½oz/100g skeins, each approx
213yd/195m (acrylic)
7 skeins in #2602 off white (C)
6 skeins in #2626 country blue (B)*

*Size I/9 (5.5mm) crochet hook
OR SIZE TO OBTAIN GAUGE*

intermediate

finished measurements

60" x 66"/152.5 x 167.5cm

gauge

One square to 16"/40.5cm using size I/9
(5.5mm) crochet hook.
TAKE TIME TO CHECK YOUR GAUGE.

stitch glossary

BL (bobble)
[Yo, pull up a lp, yo and draw through 2 lps on hook]
3 times, yo and draw through all 4 lps on hook.

square

(make 12)

With Color A, ch 5. Join with a sl st to first ch to
form a ring.

Rnd 1 (RS) Ch 4 (count as first dc and ch 1), in
ring, work [dc, ch 1] 11 times. Join with a sl st in
2nd ch of ch-4—12 dc and 12 ch-1 sps.

Rnd 2 Sl st in first ch-sp, ch 4 (count as 1 tr),
work (tr, ch 2, 2 tr) in same ch-sp (corner), *2 tr
in each of next 2 ch-1 sps, work (2 tr, ch 2, 2 tr)
in next ch-1 sp; rep from * twice, 2 tr in each of
next 2 ch-1 sps. Join rnd with a sl st to beg ch.

Rnd 3 Sl st to first ch-2 sp, ch 1, *work (2 sc, ch
2, 2 sc) in same ch-sp (corner), [sk next tr, 2 sc
in sp between next 2 tr] twice; rep from * 3
more times. Join with a sl st to beg ch—10 sc
between corner ch-2 sps. Fasten off. Turn.

Rnd 4 (WS) Join B in first ch-2 sp, ch 1, *BL, 1
sc in same ch-2 sp, [BL in next sc, sc in next sc]
5 times; rep from * 3 times. Join with a sl st to
beg ch. Turn.

Rnd 5 (RS) Sc in each st, work 3 sc in each BL
corner—11 sc between corners. Join with a sl st
to beg ch. Turn.

Rnd 6 (WS) Sc in same joining st, BL in next st,
*work (1 sc, BL, 1 sc) in corner st, [BL in next st,
sc in next st]; rep between [ ]'s to next corner;
rep from * 3 times. Join with a sl st to beg ch—7
BL between corner BL. Turn. Rep rnds 5 and 6
once—9 BL between corners. Rep rnd 5. Fasten off.

First triangle

Row 1 With RS facing, join C in 2nd sc of 3, in
any corner, ch 2, 1 hdc in each sc—22 hdc. Turn.

Row 2 Ch 2, sk first hdc, 1 hdc around post of
each of next hdc up to last, sk last hdc, 1 hdc in
turning ch. Turn.

Row 3 Ch 2, sk first hdc, 1 hdc in each hdc up
to last, sk last hdc, 1 hdc in turning ch. Turn. Rep
rows 2 and 3 until 11 rows are completed and 2
sts are left.

Row 12 Ch 2, yo, pull up a loop from post of
hdc and turning ch, yo and draw through all lps
on hook. Fasten off.

Second triangle

Join C to same sc of last hdc of row 1 of first triangle, ch 1 and rep first triangle. Make two more
triangles along other 2 sides of diamond. When
last triangle is completed, do not fasten off and
do not turn. Cont working around outside
perimeter of square as foll:

Border

Rnd 1 Work 1 sc in turning ch to the left, *16
scs along side edge of triangle, 1 sc in joining
point, 16 scs along side of next triangle, 3 sc in
corner; rep from * 3 times, end last rep with 2
sc in corner. Join with a sl st to beg ch. Fasten off.

(continued on page 140)

woven ribbons

easy

finished measurements

42" x 58"/106.5 x 147.5cm (without border)

gauges

10 sts and 12 rows to 4"/10cm over sc using size K/10½ (6.5mm) crochet hook.
One square to 6"/15cm using size K/10½(6.5mm) crochet hook.
TAKE TIME TO CHECK YOUR GAUGES.

afghan

Basic square
(make 35)
With MC ch 16.
Row 1 Sc in 2nd ch from hook and in each ch across—15 sc.
Row 2 Ch 1, turn, sc in each sc across.
Rep row 2 for a total of 18 rows. Fasten off.

long frame section

(make 16 in A and 18 in B)
With A or B, ch 36.
Row 1 Work as above—35 sc.
Rep row 2 for a total of 6 rows. Fasten off.

short frame section

(make 8 in A and 6 in B)
With A or B, ch 21.
Row 1 Work as above—20 sc.
Rep row 2 for a total of 6 rows. Fasten off.

finishing

Sew pieces tog invisibly following assembly diagram. For frame sections, position horizontal pieces with beg ch at lower edge and vertical pieces with beg ch at right edge.

Border

Rnds 1-5 Join MC with sl st in any corner. Work 100 sc evenly spaced across the top and bottom, 130 along side edges with 3 sc in each corner. Sc 1 more rnd in MC, then work 1 rnd in A and 2 rnds in MC. **Rnd 6** In corner sc, ch 3 (counts as 1 dc), dc in same sp, (ch 4, sl st in 4th ch from hook)—picot made, 2 dc in same space, *sk 3 sc, (2 dc, picot, 2 dc) in next sc; rep from * across, easing spacing so that you finish at next corner; cont around in this manner.

assembly diagram

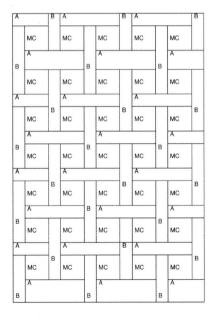

materials

Jiffy by Lion Brand Yarn Co., 3oz/85g balls, each approx 135yd/124m (acrylic)
10 balls in #153 black (MC)
4 balls in #145 plum (A)

Jiffy (multi) by Lion Brand Yarn Co.
2½oz/70g balls, each approx 115yd/103m
4 balls in #325 El Paso (B)

Size K/10½ (6.5mm) crochet hook
OR SIZE TO OBTAIN GAUGE

Large-eyed, blunt needle

prairie star

experienced

finished measurements

54" x 77"/137 x 195.5cm

gauge

One motif to 4" x 6"/10 x 15cm using size I/9 (5.5mm) crochet hook.
TAKE TIME TO CHECK YOUR GAUGE.

notes

1 After the first motif is completed, all others are joined while working rnd 3.
2 Work and join center 6 A motifs first, then work outward foll diagram.

motif I

With A, ch 4. Join with a sl st to form a ring.
Rnd 1 Ch 1, [sc, hdc, dc, tr, ch 3, tr, dc, hdc] twice all in ring. Join with a sl st in first sc.
Rnd 2 Ch 5, dc in sc,*dc in next 3 sts, (3 dc, ch 4, 3 dc) all in ch-3 sp, dc in next 3 sts**, (dc, ch 2, dc) all in next sc; rep from * to **. Join with a sl st in 3rd ch of ch-5.
Rnd 3 See note. Ch 3, *work (dc, ch 3, dc) all in ch-2 sp, dc in next 2 dc, ch 1, sk next dc, dc in next 3 dc, ch 1, sk next dc, work (3dc, ch 5, 3 dc) all in ch-4 sp, ch 1, sk next dc, dc in next 3 dc, ch 1, sk next dc **, dc in next 2 dc; rep from * to **; dc in last dc. Join with a sl st in 3rd ch of ch-3. Fasten off.

motif II

With A, work rnds 1 and 2 same as for motif I.
Rnd 3 Ch 3, dc in ch-2 sp; ch 1, with WS together sc in ch-3 sp on motif I, ch 1, dc in same ch-2 sp on motif II, dc in next 2 dc; sc in next ch-1 sp, sk

next dc on motif in progress—join made; dc in next 3 dc, join, 3 dc in ch-4 sp, ch 2, sc in ch-5 sp on motif I, ch 2, 3 dc in same ch-4 sp on motif II; complete same as motif I—one side joined.
Note Check motif placement carefully. Some motifs will be joined beg at a ch-5 sp. Some motifs will join a ch-3 sp to a ch-5 sp. Foll diagram, join all motifs as foll: sc in a corresponding sp of a completed motif (the sc replaces one ch-st on the motif in progress). Where 3, 4, or 6 points come together, join at points by sc into the sc of a previous joining.

half motif

Ch 4. Join with a sl st to form a ring.
Row 1 (RS) Ch 1, (sc, hdc, dc, tr, ch 3, tr, dc, hdc, sc) all in ring; do not join; turn.
Row 2 Ch 3, dc in first 4 sts, (3 dc, ch 4, 3 dc) all in ch-3 sp, dc in next 3 sts, 2 dc in last sc; turn.
Row 3 (joining row) Ch 3, sc in ch-sp on completed motif, ch 1, dc in first 3 dc, join, dc in next 3 dc, join, 3 dc in ch-4 sp, ch 2 sc in sc of previous joining, ch 2, 3 dc in same ch-4 sp, join to next motif, dc in next 3 dc, join, dc in next 2 dc, dc in top of ch-3, ch 1, sc in ch-sp on completed motif, ch 3, sl st in top of ch-3 of row 2. Fasten off.

finishing

Edging
Rnd 1 With RS facing, join E in any st, ch 1, work 1 rnd sc evenly around, inc at outer points and dec at inner points to keep work flat. Join to first sc. **Rnd 2** Ch 3, work 1 rnd dc, inc and dec at points as before to keep work flat. Join rnd with a sl st in 3rd ch of ch-3. Fasten off.

(see chart on page 140)

materials

Red Heart Super Saver Solids by Coats & Clark™, 8oz/226g skeins, each approx 452yd/414m (acrylic)
2 skeins in #316 soft white (F)
1 skein each in #378 claret (A) and #633 dk sage (E)

Multicolor Red Heart Super Saver by Coats & Clark™, 6oz/170g skeins, each approx 348yd/319m (acrylic)
2 skeins in #303 painted desert print (B)

Red Heart Fiesta by Coats & Clark™, 6oz/170g skeins, each approx 330yd/302m (acrylic/nylon)
3 skeins in #6013 wheat (C)
2 skeins in #6631 lt sage (D)

Size I/9 (5.5mm) crochet hook
OR SIZE TO OBTAIN GAUGE

rainbow ripple

easy

finished measuremnts

56" x 66"/142 x 167.5cm

gauge

14 sts and 14 rows to 4"/10cm over pat st using size I/9 (5.5mm) crochet hook.
TAKE TIME TO CHECK YOUR GAUGE.

afghan

With F, ch 282.

Row 1 (RS) Sc in 2nd ch from hook, sc in next ch, [sk next ch, sc in next ch, working backwards, sc in sk ch] 7 times, 3 sc in next ch, [sk next ch, sc in next ch, working backwards, sc in sk ch] 7 times, *sk next 2 ch, [sk next ch, sc in next ch, working backwards, sc in sk ch] 7 times, 3 sc in next ch, [sk next ch, sc in next ch, working backwards, sc in sk ch] 7 times*; rep from * to * across to within last 2 ch across, sc in last 2 ch. Turn.

Row 2 Ch 1, sk first sc, sc in each of next 16 sts, 3 sc in next st, sc in each of next 14 sts, *sk next 2 sts, sc in each of next 14 sts, 3 sc in next st, sc in each of next 14 sts*; rep from * to * across to within last 3 sts, sc in next st, sk next st, sc in last st. Turn. Fasten off.

Row 3 Join D in first sc, ch 1, sk first sc, sc in next st, [sk next st, sc in next st, working backwards, sc in sk st] 7 times, sc in next st, *3 sc in next st, [sk next st, sc in next st, working backwards, sc in sk st] 7 times, sk next 2 sts, [sk next st, sc in next st, working backwards, sc in sk st] 7 times*; rep from * to * across to within last 18 sts, 3 sc in next st, sc in next st, [sk next st, sc in next st, working backwards sc in sk st] 7 times, sk next st, sc in last st. Turn.

Rows 4-7 Rep rows 2 and 3 twice.
Row 8 Rep row 2. Fasten off. Turn.
Row 9 With F rep row 3.
Row 10 Rep row 2. Fasten off. Turn.
Row 11 With A rep row 3.
Rows 12-15 Rep rows 2 and 3 twice.
Row 16 Rep row 2. Fasten off. Turn.
Row 17 With F rep row 3.
Row 18 Rep row 2. Fasten off. Turn.
Row 19 With E rep row 3.
Rows 20-23 Rep rows 2 and 3 twice.
Row 24 Rep row 2. Fasten off. Turn.
Row 25 With F rep row 3.
Row 26 Rep row 2. Fasten off. Turn.
Row 27 With C rep row 3.
Rows 28-31 Rep rows 2 and 3 twice.
Row 32 Rep row 2. Fasten off. Turn.
Row 33 With F rep row 3.
Row 34 Rep row 2. Fasten off. Turn.
Row 35 With B rep row 3.
Rows 36-39 Rep rows 2 and 3 twice.
Row 40 Rep row 2. Fasten off. Turn.
Row 41 With F rep row 3.
Row 42 Rep row 2. Fasten off. Turn.
Row 43 With D rep row 3.
Rows 44-47 Rep rows 2 and 3 twice.
Row 48 Rep row 2. Fasten off. Turn.
Rows 49-168 Rep rows 9-48 3 times.
Row 169 With F rep row 3.
Row 170 Rep row 2. Fasten off.

finishing

Side edging

With RS of afghan facing, join F with a sl st in side edge of first row. **Row 1** Ch 1, making sure that work lies flat, sc in each row along side edge. Fasten off. Rep along opposite side edge.

materials

TLC Essentials by Coats & Clark™, 6oz/170g skeins, each approx 326yd/299m (acrylic)
3 skeins in #2316 winter white (F)
2 skeins each in #2220 butter (A), #2531 lt plum (B), #2672 lt thyme (C), #2772 lt country rose (D) and #2883 country blue (E)

Size I/9 (5.5mm) crochet hook
OR SIZE TO OBTAIN GAUGE

patchwork cross afghan

experienced

finished measurements

49" x 58"/124.5 x 147.5cm

gauges

16 sts and 16 rows to 4"/10cm over basic afghan st using size K/10 (6.5mm) afghan hook.
One block to 13" x 16"/33 x 40.5cm over basic afghan st using size K/10 (6.5mm) afghan hook.
TAKE TIME TO CHECK YOUR GAUGES.

block

(make 9)
With afghan hook and A, ch 45.
Row 1 (first half) Insert hook in 2nd ch from hook, yo, draw yarn through st, *insert hook in next ch, yo, draw yarn through st; rep from * to end—45 lps on hook.
Row 1 (second half) Yo, draw yarn through one lp on hook, *yo, draw yarn through 2 lps on hook; rep from * across (working backwards from left to right). **Note** One lp rem on hook and counts as first lp of next row. Rep row 1, first half and second half for basic afghan st.
Rows 2-45 Work in afghan st following chart, changing colors as indicated.
Row 46 Sl st in each vertical st across. Fasten off.
Edging
With RS facing and crochet hook, join B in upper RH corner sl.
Rnd 1 Ch 1, **sc in each of first 5 sts, *sk next st, sc in each of next 5 sts*; rep from * to * across to within last 3 sc, sk next st, sc in next 2 sc, ch 1, sc in row-end st of each row down length, ch 1**; rep from ** to ** around. Join rnd

with a sl st in beg sc.
Rnd 2 Ch 1, sc in beg sc, *ch 1, sk next sc, sc in next sc*; rep from * to* across to next corner ch-1 sp, work (sc, ch 2, sc) in corner ch-1 sp,**sc in next sc; rep from * to * across to next corner ch-1 sp, work (sc, ch 2, sc) in corner ch-1 sp**; rep from ** to ** twice more. Join rnd with a sl st in beg sc. Fasten off.
Rnd 3 With RS of block facing, join C in beg sc, ch 1, **sc in first 2 sc, dc in next corresponding sc 2 rnds below (rnd 1) pulling dc up to current level of work, sc in next sc, ch 1, sk next ch-1 sp, sc in next sc, dc in next corresponding sc 2 rnds below (rnd 1) pulling dc up to current level of work, sc in next sc*; rep from * to * across to within 3 sts from corner, ch 1, sk next ch-1 sp, sc in each of next 2 sc, work (sc, ch 2, sc) in corner ch-2 sp**; rep from ** to ** 3 times. Join rnd with a sl st in beg sc. Fasten off.
Rnd 4 With RS of block facing, join A in upper RH corner sc, ch 1, **sc in each of first 5 sts, *dc in next corresponding sc 3 rnds below (rnd 1) pulling dc up to current level of work, sc in each of next 3 sts*; rep from * to * across to next corner ch-2 sp, work (sc, ch 2, sc) in corner ch-2 sp**; rep from ** to ** 3 times. Join rnd with a sl st in beg sc.

finishing

Joining
With crochet hook and A, sl st blocks tog 3 wide by 3 long, using back lp of each corresponding st of rnd 4. When joining blocks tog, make sure that each junction of four blocks and all other corners are evenly spaced so design will not be distorted.

(continued on page 141)

materials

*Red Heart Super Saver by Coats &
Clark™, 8oz/226g skeins, each approx
452yd/414m (acrylic)
4 skeins in #313 aran (A)
2 skeins each in #633 dk sage (B)
and #631 lt sage (C)*

*Size K/10 (6.5mm) afghan hook
OR SIZE TO OBTAIN GAUGE*

Size K/10 (6.5mm) crochet hook

retro chic

It is hip to be square—updating this classic
design is made easy with new yarns
in contemporary hues.

satin granny squares

easy

finished measurements
40" x 50"/101.5 x 127cm

gauge
One motif to 4½"/11.5cm using size I/9 (5.5mm) crochet hook.
TAKE TIME TO CHECK YOUR GAUGE.

motif
(make 99)
With MC, ch 4. Join with a sl st forming a ring.
Rnd 1 (RS) Ch 3 (counts as 1 dc), work [2 dc, (ch 2, 3 dc) 3 times] in ring, ch 2. Join with a sl st in 3rd ch of ch-3. Fasten off.
Rnd 2 Join A with a sl st in any ch-2 sp, ch 3 (counts as 1 dc), work (2 dc, ch 2, 3 dc) in same ch-2 sp, *1 dc in each of next 3 dc, work (3 dc, ch-2, 3 dc) in next ch-2 sp; rep from * twice more, end 1 dc in each of next 3 dc. Join with a sl st in 3rd ch of ch-3. Fasten off.
Rnd 3 Join MC with a sl st in any ch-2 sp, ch 3 (counts as 1 dc), work (2 dc, ch 2, 3 dc) in same ch-2 sp, *ch 1, sk next 3 dc, 1 dc in each of next 3 dc, ch 1, sk next 3 dc, work (3 dc, ch 2, 3 dc) in next ch-2 sp; rep from * twice more, end ch 1, sk next 3 dc, 1 dc in each of next 3 dc, ch 1, sk next 3 dc. Join with a sl st in 3rd ch of ch-3. Fasten off.
Rnd 4 Join B with a sl st in any ch-2 sp, ch 1, work 3 sc in same sp as last sl st, *[1 sc in each of next 3 dc, 1 sc in next ch-1 sp] twice, 1 sc in each of next 3 dc, 3 sc in next ch-2 sp; rep from * twice more, end [1 sc in each of next 3 dc, 1 sc in next ch-1 sp] twice, 1 sc in each of next 3 dc. Join with a sl st in first sc. Fasten off.

Joining 2 motifs
Work rnds 1-3 of motif.
Rnd 4 Join B with a sl st in any ch-2 sp, ch 1, work 3 sc in same sp as last sl st, *[1 sc in each of next 3 dc, 1 sc in next ch-1 sp] twice, 1 sc in each of next 3*, sc in next ch-2 sp; rep from * to * once more, work (2 sc, join with a sl st in 2nd sc in corner of adjoining motif, 1 sc) all in next ch-2 sp, [1 sc in each of next 3 dc, sk next 4 sc on adjoining motif, join with a sl st in next sc of adjoining motif, 1 sc in next ch-1 sp] twice, 1 sc in each of next 3 dc, work (1 sc, join with a sl st in 2nd sc in corner of adjoining motif, 2 sc) all in next ch-2 sp; rep from * to * once more. Join with a sl st in first sc. Fasten off.

Joining 3 motifs
Work rnds 1-3 of motif.
Rnd 4 Join B with a sl st in any corner, ch 1, work 3 sc in same sp as sl st, [1 sc in each of next 3 dc, 1 sc in next ch-1 sp] twice, 1 sc in each of next 3*, work (2 sc, join with a sl st in 2nd sc in corner of adjoining motif, 1 sc) all in next ch-2 sp, [1 sc in each of next 3 dc, sk next 4 sc of adjoining motif, join with a sl st in next sc of adjoining motif, 1 sc in next ch-1 sp] twice, 1 sc in each of next 3 dc*; rep from * to * once more, work (1 sc, join with a sl st in 2nd sc in corner of adjoining motif, 2 sc) all in next ch-2 sp, [1 sc in each of next 3 dc, 1 sc in next ch-1 sp] twice, 1 sc in each of next 3 dc. Join with a sl st in first sc. Fasten off.

materials
Satin by Bernat®, 3½oz/100g balls, each approx 163yd/149m (acrylic)
5 balls in #4143 lapis (MC)
4 balls in #4141 sapphire (A)
3 balls in #4110 admiral (B)

Size I/9 (5.5mm) crochet hook
OR SIZE TO OBTAIN GAUGE

4½"/11.5cm square of cardboard

Yarn needle

(continued on page 141)

amish blocks

experienced

finished measurements
52" x 70"/132 x 178cm

gauge
One diamond motif to 3" x 5"/7.5 x 12.5cm using size I/9 (5.5mm) crochet hook.
TAKE TIME TO CHECK YOUR GAUGE.

diamond motif
First Motif
With C, ch 4. Join with sl st to form a ring.
Rnd 1 In ring work ch 1, *sc, ch 1, hdc, ch 1, dc, ch 3, dc, ch 1, hdc, ch 1, sc, ch 2; rep from * once. Join rnd with a sl st in ch-1.
Rnd 2 Sl st in ch-1 sp, work (ch 3, dc) in same sp, 2 dc in next sp, work (3 dc, ch 3, 3 dc) in ch-3 sp, [2 dc in next sp] twice, work (dc, ch 2, dc) in ch-2 sp, [2 dc in next sp] twice, work (3 dc, ch 3, 3 dc) in ch-3 sp, [2 dc in next sp] twice, work (dc, ch 2, dc) in ch-2 sp. Join rnd with a sl st in 3rd ch of ch-3—32 dc total (8 dc each side).
Rnd 3 Working in back lps only, sl st in back lp of next dc, ch 1, sk 1 dc, sl st in next dc, ch 1, sk 1 dc, *work (sl st, ch 3, sl st) in ch-3 sp, [sk 1 dc, ch 1, sl st in next dc] 4 times, ch 2**, [sl st in next dc, ch 1, sk 1 dc] 4 times; rep from * to **, end sl st in dc, ch 1, sk 1 dc, sl st in first sl st. Fasten off.
Joining motif
Referring to diagram for colors, work as for first motif through rnd 2.
Rnd 3 With RS tog and matching sides as shown on diagram, sl st in back lp of 2nd motif, sl st in front lp facing you of first motif, sk 1 dc of 2nd motif, sl st in back lp of next dc of 2nd motif, sk 1 st of first motif, sl st in next st. Cont foll diagram, matching all corners and sides.

half-motifs for top and bottom
With MC, ch 6. Join with a sl st in first ch to form a ring.
Row 1 In ring, work ch 5, dc, ch 1, hdc, ch 1, sc, ch 2, sc, ch 1, dc, ch 2, tr, ch 3. Turn.
Row 2 Work 3 dc in first sp, [2 dc in next sp] twice, 4 dc in last sp. Do not turn.
Row 3 Ch 3, working along side, sl st around side of dc, ch 1, [sl st, ch 1] twice in long sp, [sl st, ch 1] twice in ch-6 ring, sl st in long sp, ch 1, sl st around side of dc, ch 3, sl st in same sp; working along 2nd side in back lps only, [sk 1 dc, sl st in next dc, ch 1] 4 times, ch 2; working along 3rd side, [sl st in next dc, ch 1, sk 1 dc] 4 times, sl st in last sp, ch 2, sl st in same sp. Fasten off.

half-motifs for sides
With MC, ch 6. Join with a sl st in first ch to form a ring.
Row 1 In ring, work ch 1, sc, ch 1, hdc, ch 1, dc, ch 3, dc, ch 1, hdc, ch 1, sc, ch 3. Turn.
Row 2 Work 3 dc in first sp, 2 dc in next sp, (3 dc, ch 3, 3 dc) in ch-3 sp, 2 dc in next sp, 4 dc in last sp. Do not turn.
Row 3 Ch 2, working along side, sl st around dc, ch 1, sl st in next sp, ch 1, [sl st, ch 1] twice in ch-6 ring, sl st in next sp, ch 1, sl st around dc, ch 2, working in back lps only, [sl st in next dc, ch 1, sk 1 dc] 4 times, (sl st, ch 3, sl st) in ch-3 sp, [sk 1 dc, ch 1, sl st in next dc] 4 times, ch 2, sl st in same dc. Fasten off.

(continued on page 142)

materials
TLC Lustre by Coats & Clark™, 5oz/140g skeins, each approx 253yd/232m (acrylic)
6 skeins in #5017 natural (MC)
4 skeins each in #5915 claret (A) and #5861 navy (B)
3 skeins each in #5882 country blue (C), #5263 butterscotch (D), #5257 lt yellow (E), #5662 spruce (F), #5666 dk sage (G) and #5718 lt pink (H)

Size I/9 (5.5mm) crochet hook
OR SIZE TO OBTAIN GAUGE

blue crush

intermediate

finished measurements

40" x 53"/101.5 x 134.5cm

gauge

One square to 6½"/16.5cm using size G/6 (4mm) crochet hook.
TAKE TIME TO CHECK YOUR GAUGE.

stitch glossary

Long sc
Draw up a loop in center ring, bring loop up to level of row being worked, finish as for a sc.

square

(make 48)
With A, ch 5. Join with a sl st to form a ring.
Rnd 1 With A, ch 3 (counts as 1 dc), 1 dc, ch 1, 2 dc, in center of ring, *ch 3, work (2 dc, ch 1, 2 dc) in center of ring; rep from * twice more, ch 3, join with a sl st in beg dc. Fasten off.
Rnd 2 Join B in any ch-3 sp with a sl st, work (ch 3, 2 dc, ch 3, 3 dc) in same space, *ch 4, work 1 long sc in center of ring, covering ch-1 sp of previous rnd, ch 4*, **work (3 dc, ch 3, 3 dc) in next ch-3 sp; rep from * to ** twice more, and from * to * once more, join with sl st in beg dc. Fasten off.
Rnd 3 Join C in any ch-3 sp with a sl st, work (ch 3, 1 dc, ch 2, 2 dc) in same sp, *1 dc each in next 3 dc, ch 1, 1 tr in sc st of previous rnd, ch 1, 1 dc each in next 3 dc*, **(2 dc, ch 2, 2 dc)—corner made; rep from * to ** twice more, and from *

to * once more, join with a sl st in first ch-3. Fasten end off.
Note: Start working between sts with rnd 4.
Rnd 4 Join A with a sl st in any corner ch-2 sp, work 2 dc in same sp, *2 dc in next dc, 1 dc in between next 9 sts, 2 dc next dc*, **2 dc in corner sp; rep from * to ** twice more, then from * to * once, join with a sl st to beg. Fasten off.
Rnd 5 Join B with a sl st in any corner, work (ch 3, 2 dc, ch 2, 3 dc) in same corner, *ch 3, sk 2 dc of previous rnd, work 1 sc in sp before next st; rep from * to corner. **(3 dc, ch 2, 3 dc) in corner; rep from * to ** twice more and from * to ** once, ch 3, join rnd with a sl st to beg. Fasten off.
Rnd 6 Join C with a sl st in any corner, work (ch 3, 2 dc, ch 2, 3 dc) in same corner, *3 dc in each ch-3 lp of previous rnd, **(3 dc, ch 2, 3 dc) in corner; rep from * to ** twice more and from * to ** once, join rnd with a sl st to beg. Fasten off.

joining

From WS, join A with a sl st to any corner ch-2 sp of 1st square, ch 1, sc in same sp of 2nd square, *ch 1, sc in sp after next 3-dc group of 1st square, ch 1, sc in same sp of 2nd square; rep from * joining 6 squares wide and 8 squares long.

finishing

Edging
Join A with a sl st in any corner, *ch 3, sk 3 sts, work 1 sc in next space; rep from * to corner, **work (ch 3, 1 sc, ch 3, 1 sc) in corner; rep from * to ** twice more and from * to ** once more, join rnd with a sl st to beg. Fasten off.

materials

Simply Soft® by Caron®, 3oz/85g skeins, each approx 165yd/141m (acrylic/nylon)
6 skeins in #2626 dark country blue (C)
4 skeins in #2601 white (A)
3 skeins in #2624 light country blue (B)

Size G/6 (4mm) crochet hook
OR SIZE TO OBTAIN GAUGE

american star

intermediate

finished measurements

47" x 67"/119.5 x 170cm

gauge

One star motif to 5 ½"/14cm using size H/8 (5mm) crochet hook.
TAKE TIME TO CHECK YOUR GAUGE.

star motif

(make 40 using B, 41 using R and 46 using W)
Rnd 1 Ch 2, work 6 sc in 2nd ch from hook. Join with a sl st in first sc.
Rnd 2 Ch 3, in same sp work [yo and draw up a lp, yo and draw through 2 lps] 3 times, yo and draw through 4 lps on hook, *ch 5, in next st work [yo and draw up a lp, yo and draw through 2 lps on hook] 4 times, yo and draw through all lps on hook; rep from * 4 times more, end ch 5, sl st in 3rd ch of ch-3—6 clusters made.
Rnd 3 Ch 3, work 5 dc in same sp, ch 2, *work 6 dc in next ch-5 sp, ch 2; rep from * around, end sl st in 3rd ch of ch-3, ch 2, do not turn.
Rnd 4 *Dc in each dc of previous rnd, work (2 dc, ch 2, 2 dc) in ch-2 sp; rep from * around, end sl st in 2nd ch of ch-2. Fasten off.

finishing

Referring to placement diagram sew star motifs tog as shown.
Edging
Join R in any corner. Ch 3 and work one rnd of dc, dec 1 st at each V and working (2 dc, ch 2, 2 dc) in each point.

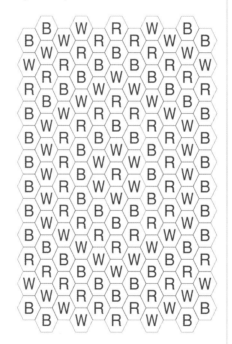

materials

Simply Soft® by Caron®, 3oz/85g skeins, each approx 163yd/150m (acrylic)
6 skeins each in #2682 red (R), #2601 white (W) and #2697 royale (B)

Size H/8 (5mm) crochet hook
OR SIZE TO OBTAIN GAUGE

harlequin diamonds

intermediate

finished measurements
49" x 63"/124.5 x 160cm

gauge
One square to 5 ½"/14 cm using size H/8 (5mm) crochet hook.
TAKE TIME TO CHECK YOUR GAUGE.

note
For every square, use one color (A through G) for rnds 1-5, then use H for rnd 6.

color sequence
With A, make 28
With B, make 24
With C, make 20
With D, make 16
With E, make 12
With F, make 8
With G, make 3

blanket square
Ch 4, join with sl st to form ring.
Rnd 1 Ch 3, 2 dc in ring, *ch 3, 3 dc in ring; rep from * twice more, ch 3, join with sl st to top of beg-ch.
Rnd 2 Ch 3, keeping last lp on hook, dc in each of next 2 dc, yo, draw through all 3 lps on hook—first corner made; *ch 4, sc in next ch-3 sp, ch 4, keeping last lp on hook, dc in each of next 3 dc, yo, draw through all 4 lps on hook—corner

made; rep from *, end last rep ch 4, sc in next ch-3 sp, ch 4, join with slip st to top of beg-ch.
Rnd 3 Ch 3, dc in same sp, *4 dc in ch-4 sp, dc into next sc, 4 dc in ch-4 sp, work (dc, ch 3, dc) in corner st of rnd 2; rep from * end last rep dc in ch-4 sp, ch 1, dc in top of beg-ch.
Rnd 4 Ch 3, dc into side of dc ending rnd 3, dc in top of beg-ch of rnd 3, dc in each of next 10 dc, *work (2 dc, ch 3, 2 dc) in corner ch-3 sp, dc in each of next 11 dc; rep from * end, 2 dc in ch-1 sp, ch 1, dc in top of beg-ch.
Rnd 5 Ch 3, dc into side of dc ending rnd 4, dc in top of beg-ch of rnd 4, dc in each of next 14 dc, *work (2 dc, ch 3, 2 dc) in corner ch-3 sp, 1 dc in each of next 15 dc; rep from * end, 2 dc in ch-1 sp, ch 3, join with sl st to beg-ch. Fasten off.
Rnd 6 Join H in any corner sp, *3 sc in same sp, 1 sc in each of next 19 dc; rep from * to end, join with sl st to first sc. Fasten off.

finishing
Holding squares as diamonds, sew tog invisibly as shown in assembly diagram.
Join H with a sl st at center st of top square; work 3 sc in this st, *work 20 sc evenly spaced along side to within 1 st of end, work this st and first st of next square tog (dec 1), work 20 sc evenly spaced along side to center st of top of next square, work 3 sc in center st; rep from * around, join with sl st to beg st. Fasten off.

materials
Wool-Ease by Lion Brand Yarn Co., 3oz/85g balls, each approx 197yd/181m (acrylic/wool)
4 balls in #170 peacock (A)
3 balls each in #148 turquoise (B), #147 purple (C) and #153 black (H)
2 balls each in #146 lilac (D) and #117 colonial blue (E)
1 ball each in #116 delft (F) and #137 fuchsia (G)

Size H/8 (5mm) crochet hook
OR SIZE TO OBTAIN GAUGE

Large-eyed, blunt needle

assembly diagram

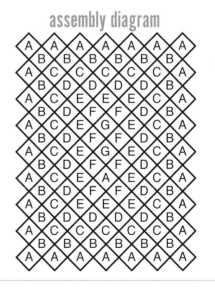

christmas rose

intermediate

finished measurements

57" x 74"/144.5 x 188cm

gauge

One flower motif to 8"/20.5cm using size J/10 (6mm) crochet hook.
TAKE TIME TO CHECK YOUR GAUGE.

strip 1

First flower motif

With A, ch 4. Join with sl st to form a ring.

Rnd 1 Ch 1, [sc in ring, ch 3] 8 times. Join with sl st to first sc.

Rnd 2 Ch 1, [work (sc, hdc, dc, hdc, sc) all in ch-3 lp] 8 times. Join with sl st to first sc.

Rnd 3 Ch 1, holding petals forward, sc in first sc of rnd 1, ch 3, [sc in next sc of rnd 1, ch 3] 7 times. Join as before. Fasten off. **Note** Always join new yarn with RS facing.

Rnd 4 Join B in any ch-3 lp, ch 1, [work (sc, hdc, 3 dc, hdc, sc) all in ch-3 lp] 8 times. Join.

Rnd 5 Ch 1, rep rnd 3 except work sc into sc of rnd 3 and ch 5 instead of ch3. Join. Fasten off.

Rnd 6 Join C in any ch-5 lp, ch 1, [work (sc, hdc, 5 dc, hdc, sc) all in ch-5 lp] 8 times. Join. Fasten off.

Rnd 7 (leaf) Join D in center dc of any petal of rnd 6; ch 2, holding back last lps on hook work 2 dc in same dc as joining, yo and through all 3 lps on hook (beg cluster made); ch 2; holding back last lps on hook, work 3 dc in same dc as joining, yo and through all 4 lps on hook—cluster (Cl) made; ch 4, [work (Cl, ch 2, Cl) all in center dc of next petal, ch 4] 7 times. Join with

a sl st in top of beg Cl. Fasten off.

Rnd 8 Join CE in any ch-2 sp, ch 1, 2 sc in same sp, *sc in top of Cl, 5 sc in ch-4 sp, sc in top of Cl**, 3 sc in ch-2 sp: rep from * around, end at **, sc in first sp. Join with a sl st in first sc.

Rnd 9 Ch 2, yo, insert hook in same sc as joining and draw lp through to height of ch, yo and draw through all 3 lps on hook (beg puff st made); ch 1; [yo, insert hook in same sc and draw lp through to previous height] twice, yo and through all 5 lps on hook—puff st (ps) made; *ch 1, sk next sc, [ps in next sc, ch 1, skip next sc] 4 times**, work (ps, ch 1, ps) all in next sc for corner; rep from * around, end at **. Join with a sl st in top of beg ps. Fasten off.

Rnd 10 Join C in ch-1 sp of any corner, ch 1, *work (sc, ch 1, sc) in sp for corner, ch 1, skip next st, [sc in ch-1 sp, ch 1 sk next st] 5 times; rep from * around. Join with a sl st in first sc.

Rnd 11 Sl st into corner ch-1 sp, ch 1, *work (sc, ch 3, sc) all in sp for corner; ch 1, [sc in next ch-1 sp, ch 3, sc in next ch-1 sp, ch 1] 3 times; rep from * around. Join. Fasten off.

Second Flower Motif

Work rnds 1-10 same as for first flower motif. Join to first motif on rnd 11 as foll:

Rnd 11 Sl st into corner ch-1 sp, ch 1, sc in sp, ch 1, sl st in corner ch-3 sp on first motif, ch 1, [sc in next ch-1 sp on second motif, ch 1] 3 times, sc in corner ch-1 sp on second motif, ch 1, sl st in corner ch-1 sp of first motif, ch 1, sc in same sp on second motif; complete as for first motif. Join. Fasten off. Cont joining motifs in this manner until there are 8 motifs in first strip. Join first motif of next strip to side of first motif of

(continued on page 143)

materials

Red Heart Classic by Coats & Clark™, 3½oz/100g skeins, each approx 198yd/182m (acrylic)
10 skeins in #917 cardinal (C)
7 skeins in #003 off white (E)
3 skeins each in #914 country red (B) and #689 forest green (D)
2 skeins #252 med coral (A)

Size J/10 (6mm) crochet hook
OR SIZE TO OBTAIN GAUGE

painted desert

finished measurements

42" x 60"/106.5 x 152.5cm

gauge

One block to 5"/12.5cm using size N/15 (10mm) crochet hook.
TAKE TIME TO CHECK YOUR GAUGE.

block

(make 70)

With A, ch 5. Join with a sl st to form a ring.

Rnd 1 Ch 3, dc in ring, ch 1, [2 dc, ch 1] in ring 7 times. Join with a sl st in 3rd ch of ch-3. Fasten off.

Rnd 2 Join B between first 2 groups of 2 dc (you will work between each of the 3 dc clusters around and through the center of the beg ring), ch 4, *(dc, ch 2, dc, ch 1) between next 2 groups of 2 dc; (dc, ch 1) between next 2 groups of 2 dc**; rep from * to ** around. Join with a sl st in 3rd ch of beg ch-4.

Rnd 3 Ch 1, sc in top of join, ch 1, sk next ch-1 sp, sc in next dc, (sc, ch 2, sc) in corner ch-2 sp, *sc in next dc, ch 1, sk next ch-1 sp, sc in next dc, ch 1, sk next ch-1 sp, sc in next dc, (sc, ch 2, sc) in corner ch-2 sp*; rep from * to * twice more; sc in next dc,

ch 1, sk next ch-1 sp. Join in beg sc. Fasten off.

Rnd 4 Join A in first sc to the left of any corner ch-2 sp, ch 1, sc in same st, *sk next sc, 2 dc in 2nd dc of corresponding dc of rnd 1, pulling up to current level of work, sc in next sc of rnd 3, 2 dc in 2nd dc of corresponding dc of rnd 1, sk next sc, sc in next sc (sc, ch 2, sc) in corner ch-2 sp **; sc in next sc*; rep from * to * twice then rep from * to ** around. Join in beg sc. Fasten off.

finishing

With A, sew blocks together in strips 7 wide by 10 long, using the back lp only of each corresponding st of rnd 4.

Border

With RS facing, join A in upper right-hand corner ch-2 sp. **Rnd 1** Ch 1, *(sc, ch 2, sc) in corner ch-2 sp, sc in each st and each ch sp on each side of joining seam across to next corner ch-2 sp*; rep from * to * around. Join in beg sc. Fasten off. **Rnd 2** Join B in beg corner ch-2 sp, (ch 5, dc) in same corner, dc in each sc around, working (dc, ch 2, dc) in each corner ch-2 sp. Join with a sl st in 3rd ch of ch-5. **Rnd 3** Ch 3, (dc, ch 2, dc) all in next corner ch-2 sp, dc in each dc around, (dc, ch 2, dc) in each corner ch-2 sp around. Join with a sl st in 3rd ch of ch-3. **Rnds 4 and 5** Ch 3, dc in each dc around working (dc, ch 2, dc) in each corner ch-2 sp. Join with a sl st in 3rd ch of ch-3. Fasten off.

materials

Red Heart Light & Lofty by Coats & Clark™, 6oz/170g skeins, each 148yd/136m (acrylic)
8 skeins in #9808 painted desert (B)
7 skeins in #9372 antique rose (A)

Size N/15 (10mm) crochet hook
OR SIZE TO OBTAIN GAUGE

nursery call

Welcome a new addition to the family
with a cuddly soft blanket
that's sure to please.

nursery throw

finished measurements

30" x 36"/76 x 91.5cm

gauge

20 sts and 26 rows to 4"/10cm over St st using size 7 (4.5mm) needles.
TAKE TIME TO CHECK YOUR GAUGE

motif A

(make 15)

**With dpn and A, cast on 155 sts (WS). Divide sts evenly between 3 needles. Turn work to RS. Taking care not to twist sts, join and place marker to indicate beg of rnds.

Rnd 1 *K5tog; turn; cast on 3 sts; rep from * around—124 sts.

Rnd 2 *With B, k2tog, k26, SKP, k1; rep from * around—116 sts.

Rnd 3 Knit.

Rnd 4 *K2tog, k24, SKP, k1; rep from * around—108 sts.

Rnd 5 Knit.

Rnd 6 With MC, *k2tog, k22, SKP, k1; rep from * around—100 sts.

Rnd 7 Knit. Cont in same manner, dec 8 sts on next rnd, then every other rnd 10 times more—12 sts.

Next rnd [SK2P] 4 times—4 sts. Cut yarn leaving a 4"/10cm tail. Thread tail into yarn needle and weave through sts. Pull tight to gather; fasten off securely.

motif B

(make 15)

With straight needles and MC, cast on 30 sts. Work in garter st for 3 rows, end with a WS row.

Row 1 (RS) Knit.

Rows 2 and all WS rows K3, p to last 3 sts, k3.

Row 3 K4, [k2tog, yo, k8] twice, k2tog, yo, k4.

Row 5 K3, [k2tog, yo, k8] twice, k2tog, yo, k5.

Rows 7, 9 and 11 Knit.

Row 13 K9, yo, SKP, k8, yo, SKP, k9.

Row 15 K10, yo, SKP, k8, yo, SKP, k8.

Rows 17, 19, 21 Knit.

Row 22 Rep row 2. Rep rows 3-17 once more. Knit next 3 rows. Bind off knitwise.

finishing

Embroidery

Using 1 strand each of A and B held tog, embroider lazy daisy in center of motif A. Using A, work French knot in center of each lazy daisy. Sew motifs tog alternating motif A and motif B, sewing motif A along rnd 2.

LAZY DAISY

FRENCH KNOT

materials

Cottontots by Bernat®, 4oz/113g balls, each approx 200yd/182m (cotton)
6 balls in #90510 sweet apricot (MC)
1 ball each in #90320 lovely lilac (A) and #90005 wonder white (B)

One pair size 7 (4.5mm) knitting needles OR SIZE TO OBTAIN GAUGE

One set (4) size 7 (4.5mm) double pointed needles (dpn), 10"/25.5cm long OR SIZE TO OBTAIN GAUGE

Stitch marker

Yarn needle

airplane blanket

intermediate

finished measurements

38" x 46"/96.5 x 117 cm

gauge

20 sts and 26 rows to 4"/10cm over St st using size size 7 (4.5mm) needles.
TAKE TIME TO CHECK YOUR GAUGE.

note

To work chart, wind each color on separate bobbins.

afghan

With circular needle and MC, cast on 170 sts. Do not join. Work back and forth in St st for 8 rows.
Beg chart I
Row 1 (RS) With MC, k83, k74 sts of chart I, reading from right to left, with MC, k13.
Row 2 With MC, p13, p74 sts of chart I, reading from left to right, with MC, p83. Cont to work as established until row 80 has been completed, end with a WS row.
Beg chart II
Next row (RS) With MC, k13, k row 1 of chart II across next 69 sts, k row 81 of chart I across next 74 sts, with MC, k14.
Next row With MC, p14, p row 82 of chart I across next 74 sts, p row 2 of chart II across next 69 sts, with MC, p13. Cont to work as established until row 92 of chart I has been completed, end with a WS row.
Next row With MC, k13, k appropriate row of chart II, with MC, k88. Cont to work as established until row 82 of chart II has been completed, end

with a WS row.
Beg chart III
Next row (RS) With MC, k13, k row 83 of chart II across next 69 sts, k row 1 of chart III across next 77 sts, with MC, k11.
Next row (RS) With MC, p11, p row 2 of chart III across next 77 sts, p row 84 of chart II across next 69 sts, with MC, p13. Cont to work as established until row 93 of chart II has been completed, end with a RS row.
Next row (WS) With MC, p11, p appropriate row of chart III, with MC, p82.
Cont to work as established to top of chart III, end with a RS row. Cont with MC only. Beg with a p row, work in St st for 7 rows. Bind off.

top and bottom borders

(make 2)
With straight needles and G, cast on 10 sts. Working in garter st, work 12 rows each in G and F. Work even until piece measures same length as width of top edge when slightly stretched, end on a row 12. Bind off.

side borders

(make 2)
With straight needles and F, cast on 10 sts. Working in garter st, work 12 rows each in F and G. Work even until piece measures same length as side edge when slightly stretched, end on a row 12. Bind off.

finishing

Sew on top and bottom borders, then sew on side borders.

(continued on page 144)

materials

Canadiana by Patons®, 3½oz/100g balls, each approx 201yd/184m (acrylic)
4 balls in #29 lt blue (MC)
1 ball each in #101 winter white (A), #5 cardinal (B), #26 mauve (C), #81 gold (D), #32 bright royal (E), #31 copen blue (F) and #120 aqua sea (G)
Small amount of #34 navy (H)

One pair size 7 (4.5mm) needles
OR SIZE TO OBTAIN GAUGE

Size 7 (4.5mm) circular needle 29"/73.5cm long

Bobbins

shell crochet baby blanket

easy

finished measurements
36" x 48"/91.5 x 122cm

gauge
16 sts to 4"/10cm over pat st using size H/8 (5mm) crochet hook.
TAKE TIME TO CHECK YOUR GAUGE.

blanket
Ch 127.
Row 1 Sc in 2nd ch from hook and in each ch across—126 sts. Ch 1, turn.
Row 2 *Sk 2 sc, dc in next sc, dc in same sc 4 times, sk 2 sc, sc in next sc; rep from * across—21 shells. Ch 2, turn.
Row 3 Dc in sc, dc in same sc twice, sc in 3rd dc at top of shell, *dc in next sc 5 times, sc in top of shell; rep from * across, end after sc in top of last shell, dc in first dc 3 times. Ch 1, turn.
Row 4 Sc in first dc, *dc 5 times in next sc, sc in top of shell; rep from * across, end on last shell. Ch 2, turn.

Row 5 Dc in sc, dc in same sc twice, sc in top of shell, *dc in next sc 5 times, sc in top of shell; rep from *, end after sc in top of last shell, dc in last sc 3 times. Ch 1, turn.
Row 6 Rep row 4.
Row 7 Rep row 5.
Rows 8-100 Rep rows 4 and 5. Fasten off.

finishing
Edging
Join yarn in upper LH corner with a sl st. **Rnd 1** Ch 1, work 199 sc evenly spaced along left side edge, 126 sc along bottom edge, 199 sc along right side edge and 126 sc along top edge. Join rnd with a sl st in first sc. **Row 1 (left side of blanket)** Sc in same st as joining, *sk 2 sc, dc 5 times in next sc, sk 2 sc, sc in next sc; rep from * across working 33 shells, end 2 sc in last sc; **(bottom of blanket)** *sk 2 sc, dc 5 times in next sc, sk 2 sc, sc in next sc; from * across working 21 shells across, end 2 sc in last sc; **(right side of blanket)** *sk 2 sc, dc 5 times in next sc, sk 2 sc, sc in next sc; rep from * across working 33 shells. Fasten off.

materials
Wintuk® by Caron®, 3½oz/100g skeins, each approx 213yd/195m (acrylic)
10 skeins in #3026 baby blue

Size H/8 (5mm) crochet hook
OR SIZE TO OBTAIN GAUGE

pastel plaid

easy

finished measurements

37" x 43"/94 x 109cm

gauge

9 sts and 14 rows to 4"/10cm over St st using size 15 (10mm) needle.
TIME TIME TO CHECK YOUR GAUGE

note

Wind each color onto separate bobbins.

blanket

·With MC, cast on 79 sts. Do not join. Work back and forth in garter st for 5 rows. Cont in pat st as foll:

Row 1 (RS) *With A, k16, with MC, k5, with B, k16*, with MC, k5; rep from * to * once more.

Row 2 *With B, p16, with MC, p5, with A, [k1, p1] 8 times*, with MC, p5; rep from * to * once more.

Row 3 *With A, [p1, k1] 8 times, with MC, k5, with B, k16*, with MC, k5; rep from * to * once more.

Rows 4-24 Rep rows 2 and 3 10 times more, then row 2 once.

Row 25 *With MC, k16, with C, k5; rep from * twice more, with MC, k16.

Row 26 *With MC, p16, with C, p5; rep from * twice more, with MC, p16.

Rows 27-30 Rep rows 25 and 26 twice more.

Row 31 *With B, k16, with MC, k5, with A, k16*, with MC, k5; rep from * to * once more.

Row 32 *With A, [k1, p1] 8 times, with MC, p5, with B, p16*, with MC, p5; rep from * to * once more.

Row 33 *With A, [p1, k1] 8 times, with MC, k5, with B, k16*, with MC, k5; rep from * to * once more.

Rows 34-54 Rep rows 32 and 33 10 times more, then row 32 once.

Rows 55 to 60 Rep rows 25 to 30.

Rows 61 to 120 Rep rows 1 to 60.

Rows 121 to 144 Rep rows 1 to 24. With MC, work in garter st for 4 rows. Bind off all sts knitwise.

finishing

Side borders

With RS facing and MC, pick up and k 92 sts evenly along side edge. Work in garter st for 4 rows. Bind off all sts knitwise. Rep on oppposite side edge.

materials

Melody by Patons®, 3½oz/100g balls, each approx 85yd/78m (acrylic)
3 balls each in #906 mint (MC) and #901 white (B)
2 balls in #908 pastel clouds variegated (A) (68% acrylic/32% nylon)
1 ball in #907 lavender (C)

Size 15 (10mm) circular needle, 36"/90cm long
OR SIZE TO OBTAIN GAUGE

Bobbins

quilted squares

intermediate

finished measurements

37½" x 46"/95 x 117cm

gauge

15 sts and 7 rows to 4"/10cm over dc using size 7 (4.5mm) crochet hook.
TAKE TIME TO CHECK YOUR GAUGE.

motif I

(make 7)
With A, ch 2.
Rnd 1 (RS) Work 8 sc in 2nd ch from hook. Join with a sl st in first sc.
Rnd 2 Ch 1, 1 sc in same sp as last sl st, *3 sc in next sc, 1 sc in next sc; rep from * twice more, end 3 sc in next sc. Join with a sl st in first sc.
Rnd 3 Ch 1, 1 sc in same sp as last sl st, 1 sc in next sc, *3 sc in next sc, 1 sc in each of next 3 sc; rep from * twice more, end 3 sc in next sc, 1 sc in next sc. Join with a sl st in first sc.
Rnd 4 Ch 1, 1 sc in same sp as last sl st, 1 sc in each of next 2 sc, *3 sc in next sc, 1 sc in each of next 5 sc; rep from * twice more, end 3 sc in next sc, 1 sc in each of next 2 sc. Join with a sl st in first sc.
Rnd 5 Ch 1, 1 sc in same sp as last sl st, 1 sc in each of next 3 sc, *3 sc in next sc, 1 sc in each of next 7 sc; rep from * twice more, end 3 sc in next sc, 1 sc in each of next 3 sc. Join MC with a sl st in first sc.
Rnd 6 With MC, ch 3 (counts as 1 dc), working in back lp only of each st to end of rnd, 1 dc in each of next 4 sc, *5 dc in next sc, 1 dc in each of next 9 sc; rep from * twice more, end 5 dc in next sc, 1 dc in each of next 4 sc. Join with sl st in 3rd ch of ch-3.

Rnd 7 Sl st in next dc, ch 4 (counts as 1 dc and ch 1), sk next dc, [1 dc in next dc, ch 1, sk next dc] twice, *work [(1 dc, ch 1) twice, 1 dc] all in next dc, [ch 1, sk next dc, 1 dc in next dc] 6 times, ch 1, sk next dc; rep from * twice more, work [(1 dc, ch 1) twice, 1 dc] all in next dc, [ch 1, sk next dc, 1 dc in next dc] 3 times, ch 1, sk next dc. Join with a sl st in 3rd ch of ch-4.
Rnd 8 Ch 3 (counts as 1 dc), [1 dc in next ch-1 sp, 1 dc in next dc] 3 times, *1 dc in next ch-1 sp, 5 dc in next dc**, [1 dc in next ch-1 sp, 1 dc in next dc] 8 times; rep from * twice more, then from * to ** once, [1 dc in next ch-1 sp, 1 dc in next dc] 4 times, end 1 dc in next ch-1 sp. Join A with a sl st in 3rd ch of ch-3.
Rnd 9 With A, ch 3 (counts as 1 dc), working in back lp only of each st to end of rnd, 1 dc in each of next 9 dc, *5 dc in next dc, 1 dc in each of next 21 dc; rep from * twice more, end 5 dc in next dc, 1 dc in each of next 11 dc. Join with a sl st in 3rd ch of ch-3.
Rnd 10 Ch 3, 1 dc in each of next 11 dc, *5 dc in next dc, 1 dc in each of next 25 dc; rep from * twice more, end 5 dc in next dc, 1 dc in each of next 13 dc. Join with a sl st in 3rd ch of ch-3.
Rnd 11 Ch 3, 1 dc in each of next 13 dc, *5 dc in next dc, 1 dc in each of next 29 dc; rep from * twice more, end 5 dc in next dc, 1 dc in each of next 15 dc. Join with a sl st in 3rd ch of ch-3. Fasten off.

motif II

(make 6)
Work as given for motif I, using B instead of A.

(continued on page 146)

materials

Baby Coordinates by Bernat®, 6oz/170g, each approx 471yd/430m (acrylic/acetate/nylon)

2 balls in #1000 white (MC)
1 ball each in #1010 soft mauve (A), #1011 lemon custard (B) and #1008 baby pink (C)

Size 7 (4.5mm) crochet hook
OR SIZE TO OBTAIN GAUGE

placement diagram

I	II	III	I
III	I	II	III
II	III	I	II
I	II	III	I
III	I	II	III

feeling ducky

easy

finished measurements
29¼" x 34"/74.5 x 86.5cm

gauge
13 sts and 20 rows to 4"/10cm over St st using size 10 (6mm) needles.
TAKE TIME TO CHECK YOUR GAUGE.

note
To work chart, wind each color on separate bobbins.

strip A
**With MC, cast on 24 sts. Work in St st for 6 rows.
Beg chart
Row 1 (RS) Cont in St st, beg chart reading row from right to left. On WS rows, read chart from left to right. Work to top of chart. With MC, cont in St st for 6 rows**.
Next row [With A, k6, with MC, k6] twice.
Next row [With MC, p6, with A, p6] twice. Rep these 2 rows for pat st. Cont in pat st until piece measures 24"/61cm from beg, end with a WS row. With MC, cont in St st for 6 rows. Work chart once more, then cont in St st with MC for 6 rows. Bind off.

strip C
Rep from ** to ** as for strip A.
Next row [With MC, k6, with A, k6] twice.
Next row [With A, p6, with MC, p6] twice. Rep these 2 rows for pat st. Cont in pat st until piece measures 24"/61cm from beg, end with a WS row. With MC, cont in St st for 6 rows. Work chart once more, then cont in St st with MC for 6 rows. Bind off.

strip B
With MC cast on 50 sts. Cont in St st as foll: *with MC, work 8 rows, with A, work 8 rows; rep from * once. Change to MC and cont in St st until piece measures 25"/63.5cm from beg. Cont in St st as foll: *with A, work 8 rows, with MC, work 8 rows; rep from * once. Bind off.

finishing

Join strips A, B and C tog; as shown.
Embroidery
Using MC, duplicate stitch eye; as shown.
Top and bottom borders
With RS facing and MC, pick up and knit 98 sts across top edge. Work in garter st for 10 rows. Bind off knitwise. Rep along bottom edge.
Side borders
With RS facing and MC, pick up and knit 148 sts across side edge. Work in garter st for 10 rows. Bind off knitwise. Rep along opposite edge.
Tassels
(make 4)
Wind MC 25 times around cardboard. Cut yarn leaving a long end, then thread end into yarn needle. Sl needle through all lps and tie tightly. Remove cardboard and wind yarn tightly around lps 1"/2.5cm below fold. Fasten securely. Cut through rem lps and trim ends evenly. Sew a tassel to each corner.

materials
Baby Bouclé by Bernat®, 4oz/113g balls, each approx 204yd/185m (acrylic/polyester)
3 balls in #103 misty blue (MC)
1 ball each in #101 soft white (A) and #104 soft yellow (B)

One pair size 10 (6mm) needles
OR SIZE TO OBTAIN GAUGE

Bobbins

4½"/11.5cm square of cardboard

Yarn needle

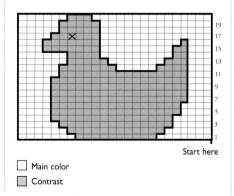

Start here

□ Main color
▨ Contrast

easy as 1-2-3

easy

finished measurements
27½" × 32½"/70 × 82.5cm

gauges
18 sts and 40 rows to 4"/10cm over garter st using size 6 (4mm) needle.
One motif to 2½"/6m using size D/3 (3.25mm) crochet hook.
TAKE TIME TO CHECK YOUR GAUGES.

center section for all blankets
With circular needle and MC, cast on 100 sts. Do not join. Working back and forth, work even in garter st until piece measures 32"/81.5cm from beg. Bind off knitwise.

apple blossom blanket
Motif I
(make 24)
With hook and MC, ch 4. Join with a sl st to form a ring.
Rnd 1 Ch 3 (counts as 1 dc), 2 dc in ring, [ch 2, 3 dc] 3 times in ring, ch 2. Join with a sl st in 3rd ch of ch-3. Fasten off.
Rnd 2 Join B with a sl st in any corner, ch 3 (counts as 1 dc), work (2 dc, ch 2, 3 dc) in same sp, [ch 1, work (3 dc, ch 2, 3 dc) in next ch-2 sp] 3 times, ch 1. Join with a sl st in 3rd ch of ch-3. Fasten off.
Rnd 3 Join A with a sl st in any corner, ch 3 (counts as 1 dc), work (2 dc, ch 2, 3 dc) in same sp, ch 1, 3 dc in next ch-1 sp, ch 1, [work (3 dc, ch 2, 3 dc) in next ch-2 sp, ch 1, 3 dc in next ch-1 sp, ch 1] 3 times. Join with a sl st in 3rd ch of ch-3. Fasten off.

Motif II
(make 24)
Work same as for motif I, using A instead of MC for rnd 1, MC instead of B for rnd 2 and B instead of A for rnd 3.

daffodil, morning glory, and wild rose blankets only
Motif I
(make 24)
With hook and A, ch 4. Join with a sl st to form a ring.
Rnd 1 Ch 3 (counts as 1 dc), 2 dc in ring, [ch 2, 3 dc] 3 times in ring, ch 2. Join with a sl st in 3rd ch of ch-3. Fasten off.
Rnd 2 Join C with a sl st in any corner, ch 3 (counts as 1 dc), work (2 dc, ch 2, 3 dc) in same sp, [ch 1, work (3 dc, ch 2, 3 dc) in next ch-2 sp] 3 times, ch 1. Join with a sl st in 3rd ch of ch-3. Fasten off.
Rnd 3 Join B with a sl st in any corner, ch 3 (counts as 1 dc), work (2 dc, ch 2, 3 dc) in same sp, ch 1, 3 dc in next ch-1 sp, ch 1, [work (3 dc, ch 2, 3 dc) in next ch-2 sp, ch 1, 3 dc in next ch-1 sp, ch 1] 3 times. Join with a sl st in 3rd ch of ch-3. Fasten off.
Motif II
(make 24)
Work same as for motif I, using B instead of A for rnd 1 and A instead of B for rnd 3.

finishing
Block center section so it measures 22½" × 27½"/56 × 70cm.
Granny square border
For top and bottom, sew 11 motifs tog, alternat-

(continued on page 146)

materials
Bumblebee by Patons®, 1¾oz/50g balls, each approx 123yd/112m (cotton)

APPLE BLOSSOM BLANKET
8 balls in #02421 apple blossom (MC)
2 balls each in #02414 wild rose (A) and #02005 lily of the valley (B)

MORNING GLORY BLANKET
6 balls in #02131 morning glory (MC)
2 balls each in #02712 sweet grass (A), #02129 blue bell (B) and #02005 lily of the valley (C)

DAFFODIL BLANKET
6 balls in #02615 daffodil (MC)
2 balls each in #02714 petunia (A), #02320 pansy (B) and #02414 wild rose (C)

WILD ROSE BLANKET
6 balls in #02414 wild rose (MC)
2 balls each in #02320 pansy (A), #02714 petunia (B) and #02005 lily of the valley (C)

Size 6 (4mm) circular needle 24"/60cm long OR SIZE TO OBTAIN GAUGE

Size D/3 (3.25mm) crochet hook OR SIZE TO OBTAIN GAUGE

go graphic

finished measurements

30" x 40"/76 x 101.5cm

gauge

24 sts and 32 rows to 4"/10cm over St st using size 5 (3.75mm) needles.
TAKE TIME TO CHECK YOUR GAUGE.

stitch glossary

M1 (make 1)

An increase worked by lifting the horizontal thread lying between the needles and placing it onto the left needle. Work this new stitch through the back loop.

square pattern

(make 12)

Beg at center with A, cast on 8 sts. Divide evenly with 2 sts on each of 4 dpns. Join, being careful not to twist, and k 1 rnd.

Rnd 2 *K2, M1; rep from * on each needle—12 sts.

Rnd 3 *K3, M1; rep from * on each needle—16 sts.

Rnd 4 *K4, M1; rep from * on each needle—20 sts.

Rnd 5 *P5, M1; rep from * on each needle—24 sts.

Rnds 6-8 Cont in this manner, p one st more before the M1 at end of each needle as before until there are 36 sts.

Rnds 9-12 With B, k one st more before the M1 at end of each needle—52 sts.

Rnds 13-16 P one st more before the M1 at end of each needle—68 sts.

Change to shorter circular needle as needed and mark for beg of rnd and incs. Cont to work 8 rnds (4 rnds k, 4 rnds p) of each color, in the following color sequence: C, D, and E; then with F, k 4 rnds and p 2 rnds. Bind off as if to purl, AT SAME TIME, mark every 47th st for ease in sewing seams.

finishing

Sew tog 3 across by 4 down.

Border

With A and longer circular needle, pick up 1 st in every st and mark each corner of afghan for inc. Work in rnds of garter st (k 1 rnd; p 1 rnd), inc as before in each corner for 9 rnds; change to B and work 2 rnds; change to F and work 2 rnds. Bind off.

materials

Babysoft by Lion Brand Yarn Co., 5oz/140g balls, each approx 459yd/420m (acrylic/nylon)
1 ball each in #157 pastel yellow (A), #156 pastel green (B), #106 pastel blue (C), #101 pastel pink (D), #144 lilac (E) and #100 white (F)

One each size 5 (3.75mm) circular knitting needles, 16"/40cm long and 36"/91.5cm long
OR SIZE TO OBTAIN GAUGE

One set (5) size 5 (3.75mm) dpn OR SIZE TO OBTAIN GAUGE

Stitch markers

Large-eyed, blunt needle

wee granny squares

beginner

finished measurements

34" x 40''/76cm x 101.5cm

gauge

One basic granny square to 7½"/19cm using size G/6 (4mm) crochet hook.
TAKE TIME TO CHECK YOUR GAUGE.

basic granny squares

First color sequence

(make 10)

With A, ch 3. Join with sl st in first ch forming a ring.

Rnd 1 (RS) Ch 3 (always counts as 1 dc), work 2 dc in ring, [ch 3, 3 dc in ring] 3 times, ch 3. Join rnd with a sl st in top of beg ch-3.

Rnd 2 Sl st over to corner ch-3 sp, ch 3, work (2 dc, ch 3, 3 dc) in same sp, *ch 1, work (3 dc, ch 3, 3 dc) in next ch-3 sp; rep from * around, end ch 1. Join rnd with a sl st in top of beg ch-3. Fasten off.

Rnd 3 With the RS facing, join B with a sl st in any corner ch-3 sp. Ch 3, work (2 dc, ch 3, 3 dc) in same sp, *ch 1, work 3 dc in next ch-1 sp, ch 1, work (3 dc, ch 3, 3 dc) in next corner ch-3 sp; rep from * around, end ch 1, work 3 dc in next ch-1 sp, ch 1. Join rnd with a sl st in top of beg ch-3.

Rnd 4 Sl st to corner ch-3 sp, ch 3, work (2 dc, ch 3, 3 dc) in same sp, *[ch 1, 3 dc in next ch-1 sp] twice, ch 1**, work (3 dc, ch 3, 3 dc) in next corner ch-3 sp; rep from * around, end last rep at **. Join rnd with a sl st in top of beg ch-3. Fasten off.

Rnd 5 With the RS facing, join C with a sl st in any corner ch-3 sp. Ch 3, work (2 dc, ch 3, 3 dc) in same sp, *[ch 1, 3 dc in next ch-1 sp] 3 times, ch 1**, work (3 dc, ch 3, 3 dc) in next ch-3 sp; rep from * around, end last rep at **. Join rnd with a sl st in top of beg ch-3.

Rnd 6 Sl st to corner ch-3 sp, ch 3, work (2 dc, ch 3, 3 dc) in same sp, *[ch 1, 3 dc in next ch-1 sp] 4 times, ch 1**, work (3 dc, ch 3, 3 dc) in next ch-3 sp; rep from * around, end last rep at **. Join rnd with a sl st in top of beg ch-3. Fasten off.

Rnd 7 With the RS facing, join D with a sl st in any corner ch-3 sp. Ch 3, work (2 dc, ch 3, 3 dc) in same sp, *[ch 1, 3 dc in next ch-1 sp] 5 times, ch 1**, work (3 dc, ch 3, 3 dc) in next ch-3 sp; rep from * around, end last rep at **. Join rnd with a sl st in top of beg ch-3.

Rnd 8 Sl st to corner ch-3 sp, ch 3, work (2 dc, ch 3, 3 dc) in same sp, *[ch 1, 3 dc in next ch-1 sp] 6 times, ch 1**, work (3 dc, ch 3, 3 dc) in next ch-3 sp; rep from * around, end last rep at **. Join rnd with a sl st in top of beg ch-3. Fasten off.

Second color sequence

(make 5)

Work as for first color sequence using D for rnds 1-2, C for rnds 3-4, B for rnds 5-6 and A for rnds 7-8.

finishing

Joining

***Join tog 5 squares of first color sequence in one long strip. With RS facing, join E with a sl st in top right corner ch-3 sp. Ch 3 (counts as 1 dc), work 2 dc in same sp, *[ch 1, 3 dc in next

materials

Babysoft by Lion Brand Yarn Co., 5oz/140g balls, each approx 459yd/420m (acrylic/nylon)
1 ball each in #157 Pastel Yellow (A), #106 Pastel Blue (B), #101 Pastel Pink (C), #156 Pastel Green (D), #100 White or colors of your choice (E)

Size G/6 (4mm) crochet hook
OR SIZE TO OBTAIN GAUGE

(continued on page 147)

clustered bobbles

experienced

finished measurements

36" x 36"/91.5 x 91.5cm

gauges

16 sts and 10 rows to 4"/10cm over pat st using size H/8 (5mm) crochet hook.
One square to 3"/7.5cm using size H/8 (5mm) crochet hook.
TAKE TIME TO CHECK YOUR GAUGES.

stitch glossary

Cl st (cluster stitch)
Ch 3, yo, insert hook in 3rd ch from hook, yo and pull up a lp, yo and draw through 2 lps on hook, [yo, insert hook in same ch, yo and pull up a lp, yo and draw through 2 lps on hook] twice, yo and draw through all 4 lps on hook.

square 1

(make 72)
With B, ch 2.
Rnd 1 (WS) [Sc, Cl st, ch 1] 4 times in 2nd ch from hook. Join with a sl st in first sc. Fasten off.
Rnd 2 With RS facing, keeping clusters on RS, join A with a sl st in any sc, ch 5 (first hdc and ch-3 sp), hdc in same sc, ch 1, [work (hdc, ch 3, hdc) in next sc, ch 1] 3 times. Join with a sl st in 2nd ch of ch-5.
Rnd 3 Ch 3 (counts as 1 dc), work (2 dc, ch 3, 2 dc) in next ch-3 sp, dc in next hdc, dc in next ch-1 sp, [dc in next hdc, work (2 dc, ch 3, 2 dc) in next ch-3 sp, dc in next hdc, dc in next ch-1 sp] 3 times. Join with a sl st in 3rd ch of ch-3. Fasten off.

square 2

(make 72)
With C, ch 6. Join with a sl st to form ring.
Rnd 1 (RS) Ch 1 (counts as 1 sc), work 15 sc in ring. Join with a sl st in first sc.
Rnd 2 Ch 2 (counts as 1 hdc), hdc in next 2 sc, [ch 3, sk next sc, hdc in next 3 sc] 3 times, ch 3. Join with a sl st in 2nd ch of ch-2.
Rnd 3 Ch 3 (counts as 1 dc), dc in next 2 hdc, work (2 dc, ch 3, 2 dc) in next ch-3 sp, [dc in next 3 hdc, work (2 dc, ch 3, 2 dc) in next ch-3 sp] twice. Join with a sl st in 3rd ch of ch-3. Fasten off.

finishing

Foll assembly chart, hold a square 1 and a square 2 tog with RS. Whipstitch pieces tog through back lps. Add squares foll chart for 12 rows of 12 squares. Whipstitch rows tog with RS facing.
Border
Rnd 1 With RS facing, join C with a sl st in any ch-3 corner sp, ch 4 (counts as 1 dc and ch 1), [dc, ch 1 in same corner] twice, *[(dc in next dc, sk next dc, ch 1) 4 times, sk seam, dc in next ch-3 sp, ch 1] across to next corner ch-3 sp, (dc, ch 1) 3 times in ch-3 sp**; rep from * to ** around. Join with a sl st in 3rd ch of ch-4. **Rnd 2** Sl st in next sp and dc, ch 4 (counts as 1 dc and ch 1), [dc, ch 1 in same corner] twice, *(dc in next ch-1 sp, ch 1) across to center dc of next 3-dc corner, [dc, ch 1 in center dc] 3 times**, rep from * to ** around. Join with a sl st in 3rd ch of ch-4.
Rnd 3 Rep rnd 2. Fasten off.
Edging
With WS facing, join D (or B for other color

(continued on page 147)

materials

TLC Baby Multicolor by Coats & Clark™, 6oz/141g skeins, each approx 372yd/341m (acrylic)
Color combinations #1 and #2
1 skein of #7956 laddie (A)
TLC Baby Solids by Coats & Clark™, 6oz/170g skeins, each approx 509yd/466m (acrylic)

COLOR COMBINATION #1
1 skein each in #7221 banana (B), #7624 lime (C) and #7812 sky blue (D)

COLOR COMBINATION #2
2 skeins in #7812 sky blue (C)
1 skein in #7221 banana (B)

Size H/8 (5mm) crochet hook OR SIZE TO OBTAIN GAUGE

sunshine floral

intermediate

finished measurements

38" x 45"/96.5 x 114.5cm

gauge

1 flower to 2½"/6.5cm wide using size H/8 (5mm) crochet hook.
TAKE TIME TO CHECK YOUR GAUGE.

stitch glossary

DC Cluster
[Yo, insert hook in st, draw through a lp, yo, draw through 2 lps] 3 times, yo, draw through 5 lps on hook.

TR Cluster
[yo twice, insert hook in st, draw through a lp, yo, draw through 2 lps, yo, draw through 2 lps] 3 times, yo, draw through 4 lps on hook.

panel

(make 5)
With A, ch 145 sts.
Row 1 (RS) [Sl st in first or next ch, sk 3 ch, 8 tr in next ch, sk 3 ch] 18 times, end sl st in last ch. Rep this row along opposite side of chain, except when making sl st, reach across to other side to insert hook, avoiding large holes between flowers—18 flowers. Cut A.
Row 2 From RS, join B, ch 4 (counts as 1 tr), [ch 2, dc cluster in 3rd tr, ch 2 dc cluster in 6th tr, ch 2, tr cluster in sl st] 18 times, end with tr in last sl st. Fasten off and rep on opposite side. Cut B.
Row 3 From RS, join C in first ch-sp, ch 3 (counts as 1 dc), 2 dc in same sp, 3 dc in each ch-2 sp across. Ch 3, turn.
Row 4 Ch 3 (counts as 1 dc), dc in each dc across. Turn.
Row 5 Ch 4, *sk 1 dc, dc in next dc, ch 1; rep from * across, end dc in last dc. Turn.
Row 6 Ch 3 (count as 1 dc), dc in each ch-1 sp and dc across. Fasten off. Using C, work rows 3-6 along opposite side.
Row 7 Panels 1 and 5, work on one side only. Panels 2, 3 and 4, work on both sides. Right side, join Color B, sc in both lps of first st, working in back lp, sc across, end sc in both lps of last st.

finishing

To join panels, hold RS tog. Join B and work sl st in back lps across. Fasten off.
Top and bottom edging
From RS, join C in upper RH corner. Making sure work lies flat, dc across top and bottom of throw, working 2 dc in each dc row, 4 dc in each ch- 4 sps, 1 tr in end of each flower row. Fasten off.
Edging
From RS, join A with a sl st in any corner. **Rnd 1** Sc around, working 3 sc in each corner st. Fasten off. **Rnd 2** From RS, join B in first sc after 3rd corner sc, sc in same st, dc, dc, sc, *sc, dc, dc, sc; rep from * around. Join with sl st in first sc. Fasten off.

materials

Wintuk® by Caron®, 3½oz/100g skeins, each approx 213yd/195m (acrylic)
4 skeins in #3256 jonquil (A)
3 skeins each in #3149 sage (B) and #3062 fisherman (C)

Size H/8 (5mm) crochet hook
OR SIZE TO OBTAIN GAUGE

cradle comforts

intermediate

finished measurements

36" x 42½"/91.5 x 108 cm

gauge

20 sts and 26 rows to 4"/10cm over St st using size 7 (4.5mm) needles.
TAKE TIME TO CHECK YOUR GAUGE.

stitch glossary

Sl 1 wyib
Sl next st purlwise with yarn at back of work.

woven pattern stitch

(multiple of 2 sts plus 1)
Rows 1 and 3 (WS) Purl.
Row 2 P1, *sl 1 wyib, p1; rep from * to end.
Row 4 P2, *sl 1 wyib, p1; rep from * to last st, end p1.
Rep rows 1-4 for woven pat st.

strip A

(make 2)
With straight needles and B, cast on 41 sts.
**With B, work in St st for 4 rows.
Beg chart II
Row 1 (RS) K10, k 20 sts of chart, reading from right to left, k11.
Row 2 P11, p 20 sts of chart, reading from left to right, p10. Cont to work to top chart, end with a RS row. Beg with a p row, work 2 rows in St st with B. With MC, work in woven pat st for 5½"/14cm, end with a WS row. With B, work in St st for 8 rows.

Beg chart III
Row 1 (RS) K9, k 23 sts of chart, reading from right to left, k9.
Row 2 P9, p 23 sts of chart, reading from left to right, p9. Cont to work to top of chart, end with a RS row. Beg with a p row, work 4 rows in St st with B**. With MC, work in woven pat st for 5½"/14cm, end with a WS row. Rep from ** to ** once more. Bind off purlwise.

strip B

(make 2)
With straight needles and MC, cast on 41 sts.
***With MC, work in woven pat st for 5½"/14cm, end with a WS row. With A, work in St st for 8 rows.
Beg chart IV
Row 1 (RS) K4, k 33 sts of chart, reading from right to left, k4.
Row 2 P4, p 33 sts of chart, reading from left to right, p4. Cont to work to top of chart, end with a RS row. Beg with a p row, work 8 rows in St st with A. With MC, work in woven pat st for 5½"/14cm, end with a WS row***. With A, work in St st for 6 rows.
Beg chart I
Row 1 (RS) K5, k 32 sts of chart, reading from right to left, k4.
Row 2 P4, p 32 sts of chart, reading from left to right, p5. Cont to work to top of chart, end with a RS row. Beg with a p row, work 6 rows in St st with A. Rep from *** to *** once more. Bind off.

(continued on page 148)

materials

Canadiana by Patons®, 3½oz/100g balls, each approx 201yd/183m (acrylic)
4 balls in #140 dk periwinkle (MC)
2 balls each in #138 periwinkle (A) and #81 gold (B)
1 ball each in #104 aran (C) and #109 brown (D)

One pair size 7 (4.5mm) knitting needles OR SIZE TO OBTAIN GAUGE

Size 7 (4.5mm) circular knitting needle 36"/90cm long OR SIZE TO OBTAIN GAUGE

counting sheep

intermediate

finished measurements

30" x 45"/76 x 114.5cm (without border)

gauge

10 sts and 12 rows to 4"/10cm over sc using size
K/10½ (6.5mm) crochet hook.
TAKE TIME TO CHECK YOUR GAUGE.

afghan

With MC, ch 76. Sc in 2nd ch from hook and
in each ch across—75 sts. Ch 1, turn.
Work in sc, following chart. When chart is
completed, fasten off.

Border

With RS facing, join MC with a sl st in any corner.
Work 73 sc evenly spaced along the top and
bottom, 100 sc evenly spaced along the sides
and 3 sc in each corner. Fasten off MC. Join C
and work 5 rnds in sc, working 3 sc in each corner, each rnd. Fasten off C. **Last Rnd** Join MC,
ch 1, work 1 sc in each of next 3 sc, *(ch 3, sl st
in first ch)—picot made, 1 sc in each of next
3 sc; rep from * around, adjusting sts so a picot
is in each corner. Join with sl st to beg ch.
Fasten off.

materials

Jiffy by Lion Brand Yarn Co., 3oz/85g balls,
each approx 135yd/124m (acrylic)
6 balls in #144 lilac (MC)
3 balls in #099 fisherman (C)
1 ball each in #124 camel (A),
#158 lemon (B), #151 oxford gray (D)
and #150 pearl gray (E)

Size K/10½ (6.5mm) crochet hook
OR SIZE TO OBTAIN GAUGE

(see chart on page 149)

on a whim

Explore your creativity and create a
stunning afghan rich in texture and color.

autumn treasure

intermediate

finished measurements
46½" x 56"/118 x 142cm

gauge
15 sts and 7 rows to 4"/10cm over dc using size I/9 (5.5mm) crochet hook.
TAKE TIME TO CHECK YOUR GAUGE.

block A
(make 15)
Large square
(make 2 for each block A).
With A, ch 9. **Foundation row (WS)** Dc in 4th ch from hook and in each ch across—7 sts. Ch 3, turn.
Row 1 Sk first st, 1 dc in next st and each st to end. Ch 3, turn. Rep row 1 once more, working ch-1 turn at end of row.
Next rnd Work 3 sc in first dc, 1 sc in each of next 5 dc, 3 sc in last st, 5 sc down side of square, work 3 sc in next corner loop of foundation ch, 1 sc in each of next 5 lps of foundation ch, 3 sc in next lp of foundation ch, 5 sc up side of square. Join MC with sl st in first sc. Cut A.
Next rnd Ch 1, 1 sc in same sp as last sl st, *3 sc in next corner sc, 1 sc in each of next 7 sc; rep from * twice more, 3 sc in next sc, 1 sc in each of next 6 sc. Join with sl st in first sc.
Next rnd Ch 3, sk first sc, 1 dc in next sc, *5 dc in next corner sc, 1 dc in each of next 9 sc; rep from * twice more, 5 dc in next corner sc, 1 dc in each of next 7 sc. Join with sl st in 3rd ch of ch-3.

Next rnd Ch 1, 1 sc in same sp as last sl st, 1 sc in each of next 3 dc, *3 sc in next corner dc, 1 sc in each of next 13 dc; rep from * twice more, 3 sc in next corner dc, 1 sc in each of next 9 dc. Join B with sl st in first sc. Cut MC.
Next rnd With B, ch 1, 1 sc in same sp as last sl st, 1 sc in each of next 4 sc, *3 sc in next corner dc, 1 sc in each of next 15 sc; rep from * twice more, 3 sc in next corner sc, 1 sc in each of next 10 sc. Join with sl st in first sc. Fasten off.

Small square 1
(make 2 for each block A)
With C, ch 6.
Foundation row (RS) Sc in 2nd ch from hook and in each ch across—5 sts. Ch 1, turn.
Row 1 Sc in each sc to end of row. Ch 1, turn. Rep row 1 3 times more.
Next rnd Work 3 sc in first st, 1 sc in each of next 3 sts, 3 sc in last st, 4 sc down side of square, 3 sc in next corner lp from foundation ch, 1 sc in each of next 4 lps of foundation ch, 3 sc in next lp of foundation ch, 4 sc up side of square. Join MC with sl st in first sc. Cut C.
Next rnd With MC, ch 1, 1 sc in same sp as last sl st, *3 sc in next corner sc, 1 sc in each of next 6 sc; rep from * twice more, 3 sc in next sc, 1 sc in each of next 5 sc. Join with sl st in first sc. Fasten off.

Small square 2
(make 2 for each block A)
Work as for small square 1 using A instead of C and D instead of MC.

Small square 3
(make 2 for each block A)
Work as for small square 1 until last rnd and
(continued on page 149)

materials
Decor by Patons®, 3 ½oz/100g balls, each approx 210yd/193m (acrylic/wool)
5 balls in #1632 rich taupe (B)
4 balls in #1662 rich bronze (C)
3 balls each in #1714 barn red (MC), #1652 deep coralberry (D) and #1657 claret (E)
2 balls in #1633 chocolate taupe (A)

Size I/9 (5.5mm) crochet hook
OR SIZE TO OBTAIN GAUGE

stars & stripes

easy

finished measurements

50" x 58"/127 x 147.5cm (not including fringe)

gauge

12 sts and 13½ rows to 4"/10cm over sc using size I/9 (5.5mm) crochet hook.
TAKE TIME TO CHECK YOUR GAUGE.

striped block

(make 10)
With C, ch 39.
Row 1 Sc in 2nd ch from hook and in each ch across—38 sc. Ch 1, turn.
Rows 2 and 3 Sc in each st across. Ch 1, turn. After row 3 is completed, join A, ch 1, turn. Working in sc, cont to work 3 rows A and 3 rows C until 13 stripes have been completed. Fasten off.
Edging
Join B in top LH corner. **Rnd 1** Ch 3, work dc in each row along side edge, work (2 dc, ch 1, 2 dc) in corner, dc in each st along bottom edge, work (2 dc, ch 1, 2 dc) in corner, dc in each row along side edge, work (2 dc, ch 1, 2 dc) in corner, dc in each st across top, work (2 dc, ch 1, 2 dc) in corner. Join rnd with a sl st in the 3rd ch of beg ch-3. Fasten off.

star blocks

(make 10)
With B, ch 39.
Row 1 Sc in 2nd ch from hook and in each ch across—38 sts. Ch 1, turn.

Beg chart
Working in sc, beg chart on row 1 and work to top. Fasten off.
Edging
Join B in top LH corner. Rep rnd 1 same as for striped block.

finishing

Sew blocks tog.
Edging
Join B in top LH corner. **Rnd 1** Ch 3, dc in each st around working (2 dc, ch 1, 2 dc) in each corner ch-1 sp. Fasten off.
Fringe
Cut one 24"/61cm long strand of A, B and C. Holding ends tog, attach in first st, *sk 2 sts and attach 3 strands in next st; rep from * across. Rep fringe on opposite edge.

materials

Simply Soft® by Caron®, 3oz/85g skeins, each approx 163yd/150m (acrylic)
8 skeins each in #2601 white (A) and #2628 dk country blue (B)
5 skeins in #2682 red (C)

Size I/9 (5.5mm) crochet hook
OR SIZE TO OBTAIN GAUGE

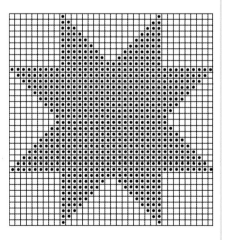

commemorative police throw

intermediate

finished measurements

44" x 64"/111.5 x 162.5cm (including border)

gauge

18 sts and 24 rows to 4"/10cm over St st using size 8 (5mm) needles.
TAKE TIME TO CHECK YOUR GAUGE.

notes

1 Afghan is worked in St st throughout.
2 Motifs are worked in duplicate stitch.

rib pattern

(multiple of 8 sts plus 4)
Row 1 (RS) K2, *p4, k4; rep from *, end p2.
Row 2 P2, *k4, p4; rep from *, end k2.
Rep rows 1-2 for rib pat.

bottom panel

Police cap
With straight needles and A, cast on 60 sts.
Work 96 rows in St st. Bind off.
Motorcycle
With circular needle and C, cast on 120 sts. Work 26 rows in St st. Change to B and cont in St st until a total of 96 rows are completed. Bind off.

middle panel

Whistle
With straight needles and D, cast on 45 sts and work 140 rows in St st. Bind off.

Police station
With straight needles and E, cast on 75 sts. Work 25 rows in St st. Change to B and cont in St st until a total of 140 rows are completed. Bind off.
Dog
With straight needles and F, cast on 55 sts. Work 36 rows in St st. Change to D and cont in St st until 140 rows are completed. Bind off.

top panel

Police car
With circular needle and G, cast on 135 sts. Work 24 rows in St st. Change to B and cont in St st until 112 rows are completed. Bind off.
Badge
With straight needles and A, cast on 45 sts. Work 112 rows in St st. Bind off.

embroidery

Using duplicate st, embroider motifs on blocks foll charts.

connecting strips

Make two 42"/106.5cm long for panels, one 16"/40.5cm long strip for bottom, two 23"/58.5cm long strips for center, and one 18"/45.5cm long strip for top as foll: with straight needles, cast on 14 sts.
Rows 1, 3, 5 and 7 (WS) K4, p6, k4.
Rows 2, 6 and 8 (RS) K1, p3, k6, p3, k1.
Row 4 K1, p3, sl next 3 sts to cn and hold in *back*, k3, then k3 from cn, p3, k1.
Rep rows 1-8 for length indicated. Referring to photo, assemble panels by sewing connecting

(continued on page 150)

materials

Wool-Ease by Lion Brand Yarn Co., 3oz/85g balls, each approx 197yd/181m (acrylic/wool)
3 balls in #107 blue heather (B)
2 balls each in #111 navy (MC), #138 cranberry (A), #189 butterscotch (D) and #151 grey heather (G)
1 ball each in #152 oxford grey (C), #403 mushroom (E), #130 green heather (H), #127 mink (I), #099 fisherman (J) and #153 black (K)

Wool-ease by Lion Brand Yarn Co., 2½oz/70g balls, each approx 162yds/146m (acrylic/wool)
1 ball in #232 woods print (F)

One pair size 8 (5mm) needles
OR SIZE TO OBTAIN GAUGE

Size 8 (5mm) circular knitting needle, 29"/73.5cm long OR
SIZE TO OBTAIN GAUGE

Cable needle (cn)

Size H/8 (5mm) crochet hook for whistle cord

commemorative fireman throw

intermediate

finished measurements

43" x 61½"/109 x 156cm (without edging)

gauge

18 sts and 17 rows to 4"/10cm over basic afghan st using size H/8 (5mm) afghan hook.
TAKE TIME TO CHECK YOUR GAUGE.

note

Each panel is worked in afghan stitch background with cross stitch embroidered motif.

stitch glossary

BAS
Basic afghan stitch

basic afghan stitch

Row 1, 1st Half Pull up lp through top lp only in 2nd ch from hook and in each ch across, keeping all lps on hook. Do not turn.
Row 1, 2nd Half Yo and pull through first lp on hook, *yo and pull through 2 lps on hook; rep from * across. Do not turn.
Row 2, 1st Half Pull up lp from under 2nd vertical "bar" of previous row and from under each vertical bar across, keeping all lps on hook. Do not turn.
Row 2, 2nd Half Rep second half of row 1.
Rep row 2 for pat st. When piece is desired length, fasten off by working sl st in each bar across.

fireman's hat

With afghan hook and B, ch 68 and work 52 rows BAS.

fire hose

With afghan hook and C, ch 117 and work 52 rows BAS.

fire hydrant

With afghan hook and A, ch 47 and work 104 rows BAS.

firehouse

With afghan hook and E, ch 67 and work 20 rows BAS. Change to C and work 84 rows BAS—104 rows total.

dalmation

With afghan hook and A, ch 62 and work 104 rows BAS.

fire truck

With afghan hook and E, ch 127 and work 10 rows BAS. Change to C and work 60 rows BAS—70 rows total.

fire alarm

With afghan hook and B, ch 58 and work 70 rows BAS.

(continued on page 153)

materials

*Wool-Ease by Lion Brand Yarn Co.,
3oz/85g balls, each approx
197yd/181m (acrylic/wool)
7 balls in #107 blue heather (C)
5 balls in #138 cranberry (D)
4 balls in #189 butterscotch (A)
3 balls in #151 grey heather (B)
2 balls in #152 oxford grey (E)
1 ball each in #099 fisherman (F)
and #153 black (G)*

---

*Size H/8 (5mm) flexible afghan hook
OR SIZE TO OBTAIN GAUGE*

Size H/8 (5mm) crochet hook

Large-eyed, blunt needle

country santa throw

experienced

finished measurements

52" x 62"/132 x 157.5cm

gauge

16 sts and 14 rows to 4"/10cm over basic afghan st using size J/10 (6mm) afghan hook.
TAKE TIME TO CHECK YOUR GAUGE.

block A

(make 16)
Using afghan hook and B, ch 11.
Basic afghan stitch
Row 1 first half Insert hook into 2nd ch from hook, (working from right to left) yo, draw yarn through st, (insert hook in next ch, yo, draw through st) across—11 lps on hook.
Row 1 second half Yo, draw yarn through one lp on hook, *yo, draw yarn through 2 lps on hook; rep from * across (working backwards from left to right). **Note** One lp rem on hook and counts as first loop of next row. Rep row 1(first half and second half) until there are 11 rows.
Row 12 Sl st in each vertical st (or "bar") across—11 sts each row. Fasten off.

block B

(make 12)
Using afghan hook and C, ch 51. Rep row 1 of block A over 51 sts.
Rows 2-51 Foll chart for block B, work in afghan stitch changing colors where indicated.
Row 52 Rep row 12 of block A.

block C

(make 12)
Using afghan hook and CC, ch 11. Rep row 1 of block A over 11 sts.
Rows 2-51 Foll chart for block C, work in afghan stitch changing colors where indicated.
Row 52 Rep row 12 of block A.

block D

(make 5)
Using afghan hook and C, ch 51. Rep row 1 of block A over 51 sts.
Rows 2-51 Foll chart for block D, work in afghan stitch changing colors where indicated.
Row 52 Rep row 12 of block A over 51 sts.
Embroidery
Follow cross-stitch chart for back-stitch and cross-stitch design for block D (santa) squares.

block E

(make 4)
Using afghan hook and C, ch 51. Rep row 1 of block A over 51 sts.
Rows 2-51 Work even in afghan stitch.
Row 52 Rep row 12 of block A over 51 sts.

finishing

Using C, sl st blocks tog following assembly diagram, using back lp of each corresponding st on edge of block. When joining blocks together, make sure that each junction of four blocks, and all other corners, are evenly spaced so design will not be distorted.

(continued on page 156)

materials

Red Heart Super Saver by Coats & Clark™, 6oz/170g skeins, each approx 348yd/319m (acrylic)
2 skeins in #4313 aran fleck (A)
Red Heart Super Saver by Coats & Clark™, 8oz/226g skeins, each approx 452yd/414m (acrylic)
6 skeins in #633 dk sage (C)
2 skeins in #376 burgundy (B)
1 skein each in #334 buff (D),
#341 lt grey (E) and #312 black (F)

Size J/10 (6mm) afghan hook
OR SIZE TO OBTAIN GAUGE

Size I/9 (5.5mm) crochet hook

falling leaves

intermediate

finished measurements

46" x 64"/117 x 162.5cm

gauge

13 sts and 8 rows to 4"/10cm over dc using size
size H/8 (5mm) crochet hook.
TAKE TIME TO CHECK YOUR GAUGE.

panel

(make 4)

With A, ch 41. **Row 1(RS)** Dc in 4th ch from
hook, dc in next 2 ch, ch 1, sk next 3 sts, dc in next
st, ch 1, dc in 2nd sk st, ch 1, sk next st—extended
cross stitch made (xcs) worked over 5 sts; dc in
next 2 ch, ch 1, sk next ch, dc in next 15 ch, ch 1,
sk next ch, dc in next 2 ch, xcs, dc in last 4 ch. Turn.
Rows 2-113 Ch 3, dc in next 3 sts, xcs, dc in next
2 sts, ch 1, sk next st, dc in next 15 sts, ch 1, dc in
next 2 sts, xcs, dc in last 4 sts. Turn. Fasten off.

leaf

(make 16 for each panel)

Using desired leaf color (B through H), and leaving a 6"/15cm strand at slip knot on end of hook,
ch 8. **Rnd 1** Work 3 dc in 4th ch from hook, hdc
in next 2 ch, sc in next ch, 3 sc in last ch; working on opposite side of beg ch, sc in next ch, hdc
in next 2 ch, 3 dc in same ch as first 3 dc. Join
with a sl st in top of ch-3—16 sts.
Rnd 2 Ch 1, 2 sc in same ch as joining, [2 sc in
next dc] 3 times, sc in next 4 sts, work (2 sc, ch
2 sl st in top and side lps of last sc, sc) in next sc,

sc in next 4 sts, [2 sc in next dc] 3 times. Join to
first sc, ch 6, sl st in 2nd ch from hook and each
ch, sl st in next sc on leaf. Fasten off.

assembly

Randomly sew desired leaf colors to panels as
shown or as desired. We placed leaves every six
to seven rows.

Panel edging

Rnd 1 With B (or color of choice), join at top
left side bar of last worked row, ch 4, *dc over
bar of next row end, ch 1; rep from * to corner,
work (dc, ch 3, dc) all in last st for corner; working on opposite side of ch, **ch 1, sk 1, dc in next
dc; rep from ** to next corner; rep from *
around. Join with a sl st in 3rd ch of ch-4.
Rnd 2 Sl st into ch-1 sp, ch 4, *dc in next dc, ch
1; rep from * working (dc, ch-3, dc) in corner ch-
3 sp. Join with a sl st in 3rd ch of ch-4.

second panel

Work same as for first panel through until rnd 1
has been completed. Work rnd 2 down the first
long side and across the bottom to the corner.
Panels are joined with sl sts in corresponding ch-
1 sps along each side. Where corners meet, join
corners by working dc, ch 1 (in first panel), sc in
ch-3 sp of 2nd panel, ch 1, dc in same ch-3 sp of
first panel, ch 1, cont as established.
Rnd 2 (joining rnd) With RS facing, beg at the
corner, dc, ch 1 in first panel, sc in ch-3 corner sp
of second panel, ch 1, dc in ch-3 corner sp of first
panel, *sl st in ch-1 sp of second panel, dc in next
dc of first panel; rep from * around. Join other

(continued on page 157)

materials

Red Heart Tweed by Coats & Clark™,
4oz/114g skeins, each approx
222yd/203m (acrylic)
9 skeins in #7071 Irish coffee (A)
Super Saver by Red Heart, 8oz/226g
skeins, each approx 452yd/414m (acrylic)
1 skein each in #330 linen (B)
and #661 frosty green (C)
Red Heart Classic by Coats & Clark™,
3½oz/100g skeins, each approx
198yd/182m (acrylic)
1 skein each in #289 copper (D),
#286 bronze (E), #365 coffee (F),
#254 pumpkin (G) and
#644 dk sage (H)

Size H/8 (5mm) crochet hook
OR SIZE TO OBTAIN GAUGE

summer shells

experienced

finished measurements

49" x 63"/124.5 x 160cm

gauge

8 sts and 14 rows to 4"/10cm over basic afghan st using size H/8 (5mm) afghan hook.
TAKE TIME TO CHECK YOUR GAUGE.

note

Afghan squares are worked in basic afghan stitch with worked-in chart pattern and applied borders.

basic afghan stitch

With afghan hook, ch number of sts indicated.
First half row Insert hook into 2nd ch from hook, (working from right to left) yo, draw yarn through st, *insert hook in next ch, yo, draw through st; rep from * across.
Second half row Yo, draw yarn through one lp on hook, *yo, draw yarn through 2 lps on hook; rep from * across (working backwards from left to right). **Note** One lp rem on hook and counts as first lp of next row.

center square

(make 12)
With afghan hook and MC, ch 32. Work 26 rows in basic afghan stitch. At end, sl st across in each bar to close—26 rows. Fasten off.

Edging

With crochet hook, join MC with a sl st in upper right corner *hdc in each st across, 3 hdc in corner st, hdc in ea row end, 3 hdc in corner st; rep from * once. Join with a sl st in first hdc. Fasten Off.

charted squares

(make 18)
Make 3 foll chart #1, 2 foll chart #2, 2 foll chart #3, 3 foll chart #4, 2 foll chart #5, 3 foll chart #6 and 3 foll chart #7. Foll each chart reading from right to left and bottom to top, or invert chart for a different angle; as shown in photo. With afghan hook and A, ch 32. Work chart rows in basic afghan stitch. At end, sl st across in each bar to close—26 rows. Fasten off.

Edging

Work as for center square.

finishing

Joining

Foll photo for placement, place 2 squares tog WS facing. With crochet hook, join MC in outer lps of both pieces in corner hdc, sl st through both lps, *ch 1, sl st through both lps of next hdc; rep from * to end. Fasten off. Join 5 squares in each row placing solid squares in center. Join rows of 5 squares in same manner for 6 strips of 5 row squares.

Border

Row 1 With RS side facing and crochet hook, join MC with a sl st in upper right corner; hdc evenly spaced around, working 3 hdc in each corner. Join rnd with a sl st in first hdc. Fasten off.
Rnd 2 Join B with a sl st in hdc before 3-hdc corner, ch 3, dc in next hdc, sk next hdc, dc in next

(continued on page 158)

materials

Red Heart Super Saver by Coats & Clark™, 8oz/226g skeins, each approx 452yd/414m (acrylic)
5 skeins in #316 soft white (MC)
2 skeins in #382 country blue (A)
Red Heart Fiesta by Coats & Clark™, 6oz/170g skeins, each approx 330yd/302m (acrylic/nylon)
1 skein in #6301 baby white (B)

Size H/8 (5mm) flexible afghan hook, 22"/56cm long OR
SIZE TO OBTAIN GAUGE

Size H/8 (5mm) crochet hook

approx approximately

beg begin(ning)

bind off Used to finish an edge and keep stitches from unraveling. Lift the first stitch over the second, the second over the third, etc. (UK: cast off)

cast on A foundation row of stitches placed on the needle in order to begin knitting.

CC contrast color

ch chain(s)

cm centimeter(s)

cont continu(e)(ing)

dc double crochet (UK: tr–treble)

dec decrease(ing)–Reduce the stitches in a row (knit 2 together).

dpn double-pointed needle(s)

dtr double treble (UK: trtr—triple treble)

foll follow(s)(ing)

g gram(s)

garter stitch Knit every row. Circular knitting: knit one round, then purl one round.

grp(s) group(s)

hdc half double crochet (UK: htr–half treble)

inc increase(ing)–Add stitches in a row (knit into the front and back of a stitch).

k knit

k2tog knit 2 stitches together

LH left-hand

lp(s) loop(s)

m meter(s)

M1 make one stitch–With the needle tip, lift the strand between last stitch worked and next stitch on the left-hand needle and knit into the back of it. One stitch has been added.

MC main color

mm millimeter(s)

no stitch On some charts, "no stitch" is indicated with shaded spaces where stitches have been decreased or not yet made. In such cases, work the stitches of the chart, skipping over the "no stitch" spaces.

oz ounce(s)

p purl

p2tog purl 2 stitches together

pat(s) pattern

pick up and knit (purl) Knit (or purl) into the loops along an edge.

pm place markers–Place or attach a loop of contrast yarn or purchased stitch marker as indicated.

psso pass slip stitch(es) over

rem remain(s)(ing)

rep repeat

rev St st reverse stockinette stitch–Purl right-side rows, knit wrong-side rows. Circular knitting: purl all rounds. (UK: reverse stocking stitch)

rnd(s) round(s)

RH right-hand

RS right side(s)

sc single crochet (UK: dc–double crochet)

sk skip

SKP Slip 1, knit 1, pass slip stitch over knit 1.

SK2P Slip 1, knit 2 together, pass slip stitch over the knit 2 together.

sl slip–An unworked stitch made by passing a stitch from the left-hand to the right-hand needle as if to purl.

sl st slip stitch (UK: sc–single crochet)

sp(s) space(s)

ssk slip, slip, knit–Slip next 2 stitches knitwise, one at a time, to right-hand needle. Insert tip of left-hand needle into fronts of these stitches from left to right. Knit them together. One stitch has been decreased.

sssk Slip next 3 sts knitwise, one at a time, to right-hand needle. Insert tip of left-hand needle into fronts of these stitches from left to right. Knit them together. Two stitches have been decreased.

st(s) stitch(es)

St st Stockinette stitch–Knit right-side rows, purl wrong-side rows. Circular knitting: knit all rounds. (UK: stocking stitch)

tbl through back of loop

t-ch turning chain

tog together

tr treble (UK: dtr—double treble)

trtr triple treble (UK: qtr—quadruple treble)

WS wrong side(s)

wyib with yarn in back

wyif with yarn in front

work even Continue in pattern without increasing or decreasing. (UK: work straight)

yd yard(s)

yo yarn over–Make a new stitch by wrapping the yarn over the right-hand needle. (UK: yfwd, yon, yrn)

* = Repeat directions following * as many times as indicated.

[ ] = Repeat directions inside brackets as many times as indicated.˘

crochet ripple

(continued from page 12)

work 4 sc in ch-2 sp of ascending point, [1 sc in each of next 2 dc, working over ch, work 1 dc in each of 2 sk dc] twice, 1 sc in next dc, draw up a lp in each of next 2 dc over descending point, yo and draw through all 3 lps for dec; rep from * across, ending last rep by drawing up a lp in each of last dc and in 3rd ch of turning-ch, yo and draw through all 3 lps. Fasten off.

Finishing row on lower edge

From RS, join A with a sl st in 2nd ch of beg-ch in first point at right corner of lower edge, ch 1, work 1 sc in same ch as joining, 1 sc in next ch-1 sp; working along opposite side of base-ch, *work 1 sc in each of next 8 ch, draw up a lp in each of next 3 ch over descending point, yo and draw through all 4 lps on hook for dec, 1 sc in each of next 8 ch, work 4 sc in ch-2 sp of ascending point; rep from * across, ending last rep with 1 sc in ch-1 sp, 1 sc in first base-ch. Fasten off.

finishing

Steam lightly on WS.

prairie stripes

(continued from page 24)

side edge, work 3 sc in top right corner—482 sts. Join rnd with a sl st in first sc. Rnds 2 and 3 Ch 1, sc in each st around, working 3 sc in center st of each corner. Join rnd with a sl st in first sc. When rnd 3 is completed, join rnd with a sl st in first sc changing to B. Rnds 4-7 With B, rep rnd 2. When rnd 7 is completed, join rnd with a sl st in first sc changing to D. Rnds 8-11 With D, rep rnd 2. When rnd 11 is completed, fasten off.

double diamond throw

(continued from page 34)

sc) twice, Psc] twice, sc in next 12; rep between *'s, sc in 2; rep between **'s, sc in 2; rep between *'s, sc in last st. Ch 1, turn.

Row 16 Sc in first st, *tr, sk 1, sc, tr, sk 1*, sc, **dc, sk 1, work 5 sc, dc around marked st in 2nd row below, sk 1, sc, dc around same marked st, sk 1, work 5 sc, dc, sk 1**, sc; rep between *'s, sc in 11, Psc, [sc, Psc] 3 times, work [sc in 11; rep between **'s, sc in 11, (Psc, sc) 3 times, Psc] twice, sc in 11; rep between *'s, sc; rep between **'s, sc; rep between *'s, sc in last sc. Ch 1, turn.

Row 18 Sc in first st, *tr, sk 1, sc, tr, sk 1, *sc in next 2, **dc, sk 1, [work 3 sc, dc, sk 1] 3 times, **sc in next 2; rep between *'s, sc in 10, Psc, [sc, Psc] 4 times, work [sc in 11; rep between **'s, sc in 11, (Psc, sc) 4 times, Psc] twice, sc in 10; rep between *'s, sc in 2; rep between **'s, sc in 2, rep between *'s. Ch 1, turn.

Row 20 Sc in first st, *tr, sk 1, sc, tr, sk 1, *sc in next 3, **dc, sk 1, work 1 sc, dc, sk 1, 5 sc, dc, sk 1, 1 dc, sk 1, **sc in next 3; rep between *'s, sc in 9, Psc, [sc, Psc] 5 times, [sc in 11, rep between **'s, sc in 11, (Psc, sc) 5 times, Psc] twice, sc in 9; rep between *'s, sc in next 3; rep between **'s, sc in 3; rep between *'s, sc. Ch 1, turn.

Row 22 Sc in first st, *tr, sk 1, sc, tr, sk 1, sc in next 4, **work dec dc as foll: yo, insert hook under next dc, yo, draw up lp, yo, draw through 2 lps, yo, insert hook under next dc, yo, draw up lp, yo, draw through 2 lps, yo, draw through 3 lps, sk 1, sc in 7, work dec dc**, sc in 4; rep between *'s, sc in 8, Psc, [sc, Psc] 6 times, [sc in 11; rep between **'s, sc in 11, (Psc, sc) 6 times, Psc] twice, sc in 8; rep between *'s, sc in 4; rep between **'s, sc in 4, rep between *'s, sc. Ch 1, turn.

Row 24 Sc in first st, *tr, sk 1, sc, tr, sk 1, *sc in 3, **dc around 2nd half of dec dc, sk next sc, sc, work dc around first half of dec dc, sk 1, work 5 sc, dc around 2nd half of dec dc, sk 1, sc, working under post, dc in dec dc in 2 rows below, sk 1, **sc in next 3; rep between *'s, sc in 9, Psc, [sc, Psc] 5 times, [sc in 11, rep between **'s, sc in 11, (Psc, sc) 5 times, Psc] twice, sc in 9; rep between *'s, sc in 3; rep

between **'s, sc in 3; rep between *'s, sc. Ch 1, turn.

Row 26 Rep row 18.

Row 28 Sc in first st, *tr, sk 1, sc, tr, sk 1*, sc, **dc, sk 1, 5 sc, dc, sk 1, sc, dc, sk 1, 5 sc, dc, sk 1, **sc; rep between *'s, sc in 11, Psc, [sc, Psc] 3 times, [sc in 11, rep between **'s, sc in 11, (Psc, sc) 3 times, Psc] twice, sc in 11; rep between *'s, sc; rep between **'s, sc; rep between *'s, sc. Ch 1, turn.

Row 30 Sc in first st, *tr, sk 1, sc, tr, sk 1, *sc in 2, **dc, sk 1, 5 sc, work dec dc as in row 22, sk 1, sc in 5, dc, sk 1, **sc in 2; rep between *'s, sc in 12, Psc, [sc, Psc] twice, [sc in 13; rep between **'s, sc in 13, (Psc, sc) twice, Psc] twice, sc in 12; rep between *'s, sc in 2; rep between **'s, sc in 2; rep between *'s, sc. Ch 1, turn.

Row 32 Rep row 12.

Row 34 Rep row 10.

Row 36 Rep row 8.

Row 38 Rep row 6.

Row 40 Sc, *tr, sk 1, sc, tr, sk 1*, sc in 7, **dc, sk 1, sc, dc, sk 1**, sc in 7, rep between *'s, sc in 35; rep between **'s, sc in 41; rep between **'s, sc in 35; rep between *'s, sc in 7; rep between **'s, sc in 7; rep between *'s, sc. Ch 1, turn.

Row 42 Sc, *tr, sk 1, sc, tr, sk 1*, sc in 8, dec dc as on row 22, sc in 8; rep between *'s, sc in 36, dec dc, sc in 43, dec dc, sc in 36; rep between *'s, sc in 8, dec dc, sc in 8; rep between *'s, sc. Ch 1, turn.

Row 44 Sc, *tr, sk 1, sc, tr, sk 1*, sc in 9, mark last st, sc in 8, rep between *'s, sc in 37, mark last st, sc in 44, mark last st, sc in 36, rep between *'s, sc. Ch 1, turn. Rep rows 3-44 5 times, working tr on row 3 and end with row 3.

finishing

Left and right side edging

Work in ends of rows. From RS with smaller hook, sl st in first st, *Psc in next st, sl st, rep from * across.

Lattice Fringe

Row 1 From RS, join yarn in first sc, ch 1, insert hook in back of lp of ch just made, sc in ch (Double chain made—Dch); work 2 more Dch, *sk 3, sc in

double diamond throw

(continued from page 135)

next st, 3 Dch; rep from * across, end sc in last st. Turn. **Row 2** *Work 3 Dch, sc in ch sp; rep from * across. Turn. **Row 3** Rep row 2. Fasten off.

Fringe

Cut 5 16"/40.5cm long strands. Work on WS of afghan. Holding 5 strands tog, fold in half, pull lp through 3 Dch sp, pull ends up and tighten.

alaskan nights

(continued from page 38)

Row 23 Sc in each sc and in each ch-1 sp across, ending by working sc in turning ch sp, ch 1, turn.

Row 24 Sc in each sc across, ch 1, turn.

Row 25 (WS) Sc in each of first 3 sc, *attach ch-7 as foll: insert hook in next sc and then in back ridge of center of ch of ch-7; hook yarn, draw lp through and complete st as a sc, sc in each of next 5 sc*; rep from * to * across, ending last rep by working sc in each of last 3 sc, ch 1, turn.

Rows 26-30 Sc in each sc across, ch 1, turn, end of row 30, do not turn.

Rows 31-105 Rep rows 6-30 3 times.

Rows 106–117 Rep rows 6-17, end of row 117, do not turn, do not fasten off, work border.

Border

Rnd 1 With RS facing, working across width, ch 3 (first dc), *[dc in row-end st of next 15 rows, sk next row] 6 times, dc in each of last 6 dc across to corner, ch 2, working down length, dc in each sc across to next corner, ch 2*, dc in first row-end st of first row across width; rep from * to * around, join with sl st to top of beg ch 3. Fasten off.

floral water lily

(continued from page 40)

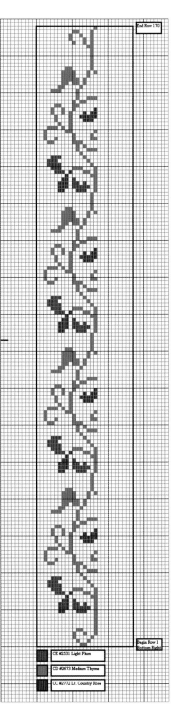

CE #2531 Light Plum
CD #2673 Medium Thyme
CC #2772 Lt. Country Rose

open windows set

(continued from page 44)

finishing

Referring to diagram, sew panels tog, alternating them as shown.

Edging

From RS with circular needle and MC, pick up and k 330 sts evenly along each side edge. Knit next 2 rows. Bind off.

Fringe

For each fringe, cut strands 10"/25.5cm long. Holding 3 strands tog and matching colors at end of each panel as shown, knot fringe evenly spaced across top and bottom edges.

pillow

(back and front make alike.)

With straight needles and MC, cast on 22 sts, with A, cast on 44 sts, with MC, cast on 22 sts—88 sts.
Row 1 (RS) With MC, k22, with A, k44, with MC, k22.
Row 2 With MC, p22, with A, k44, with MC, p22.
Row 3 With MC, k22, with A, [k1, p1] 22 times, with MC, k22.
Rep rows 2 and 3 12 times more, then row 2 once.**
Row 4 With A, k22, with MC, k44, with A, k22.
Row 5 With A, k22, with MC, p44, with A, k22.
Row 6 With A, [k1, p1] 11 times, with MC, k44, with A, [k1, p1] 11 times.
Rep rows 5 and 6 5 times more, then row 5 once.
Row 7 With A, [k1, p1] 11 times, with MC, k12, with A, k20, with MC, k12, with A, [k1, p1] 11 times.
Row 8 With A, k22, with MC, p12, with A, [k2, p2] 5 times, with MC, p12, with A, k22.
Row 9 With A, [k1, p1] 11 times, with MC, k12, with A, [k2, p2] 5 times, with MC, k12, with A, [k1, p1] 11 times.

Row 10 With A, k22, with MC, p12, with A, [p2, k2] 5 times, with MC, p12, with A, k22.
Row 11 With A, [k1, p1] 11 times, with MC, k12, with A, [p2, k2] 5 times, with MC, k12, with A, [k1, p1] 11 times.
Rep rows 8-11 5 times more, then rows 8 and 9 once.
Row 12 With A, k22, with MC, p44, with A, k22.
Row 13 With A, [k1, p1] 11 times, with MC, k44, with A, [k1, p1] 11 times.
Rep rows 12 and 12 6 times more, then rows 12 once. Rep from ** to ** once more. Bind off in pat st.

finishing

Sew pieces tog along all but bottom edge. Insert pillow form; sew bottom edge closed.

Panel 1   Panel 2   Panel 1   Panel 2   Panel 1

lacy fern afghan

(continued from page 46)

finishing

Weave k1 edge of left panel to k1 edge of center panel. Rep for right panel.

Border

Row 1 With RS facing, sc evenly in each st across end to first point, ch 1, *sc in 15 sts, sc in center st of "V", sc in 15 sts to next point, ch 1; rep from * across to last point, sc evenly to edge. Turn. **Row 2** Ch 1 (for dc, ch 1), [sk 1 st, dc in next st] to 2 sts before first point, *sk 1 st, [dc, ch 1, dc] in next st, ch 1, dc in ch 1 sp; ch 1, [dc, ch 1, dc] in first of 15 sc, [sk 1 sc, dc in next sc] 6 times, sk 1 sc, center dec over next 3 sts, [sk 1 sc, dc in next sc] 6 times; rep from * across to last point, end [sk 1 st, dc in next st] across to last st. Fasten off.

handloomed homespun

(continued from page 48)

side edge of afghan, however, picking up 144 sts instead of 108 sts. Join border corners with flat seam. Weave in ends.

afghan panels

1	2	3	4	5	6
A	C	E	A	C	B
B	D	A	D	B	E
C	E	B	C	A	D
D	A	C	B	E	C
E	B	D	A	D	B
B	C	A	E	C	A

octagon afghan

(continued from page 56)

other octagons along side edges. Use one color marker for incs and another for decs.

Top and bottom edges

*With circular needle and CC, pick up and k16 sts across side of octagon on top edge, place inc marker, rep from * once, pick up and k16 sts across next side of octagon, place dec marker, rep placement of 2 inc markers, one dec marker 2 (5) more times across edge, end by placing 2 inc markers, pick up and k16 sts to end of row. **Next row (WS)** Knit. **Next row (RS)** Inc 1 st in first st of row, k to st before inc marker, inc 1 st in st before and inc 1 st in st after marker—2 sts made, cont across row, making incs before and after each inc marker and working to 2 sts before dec marker, k2tog before dec marker, k2tog after dec marker, cont across row working incs and decs where indicated, inc in last st of row. **Next row (WS)** Knit. Rep incs and decs on RS rows, k16 rows (8 ridges) of CC, 4 rows of MC, binding off across last WS row of MC. Rep for bottom edge.

Side edges

Pick up and k16 sts along one side of octagon, place inc marker, pick up and k16 sts along next side of octagon, place dec marker, [place 2 inc markers, 1 dec marker] 3 (5) times, ending placing 1 inc marker, work 16 sts to end of row. Work remainder of edging as for top edge. Rep for other side edge. Sew edging seams with flat seam. Weave in ends.

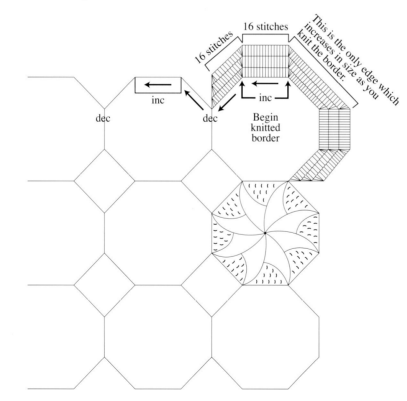

garden sprinkling can

(continued from page 60)

Edging
Rnd 1 From RS with crochet hook, join MC in upper right corner; ch 1, sc evenly spaced around, working 3 sc in each corner. Join with a sl st in first sc. Turn. **Rnd 2** Ch 1, *sc in next sc, bead st in next sc; rep from * around. Join with a sl st in first sc. Fasten off.

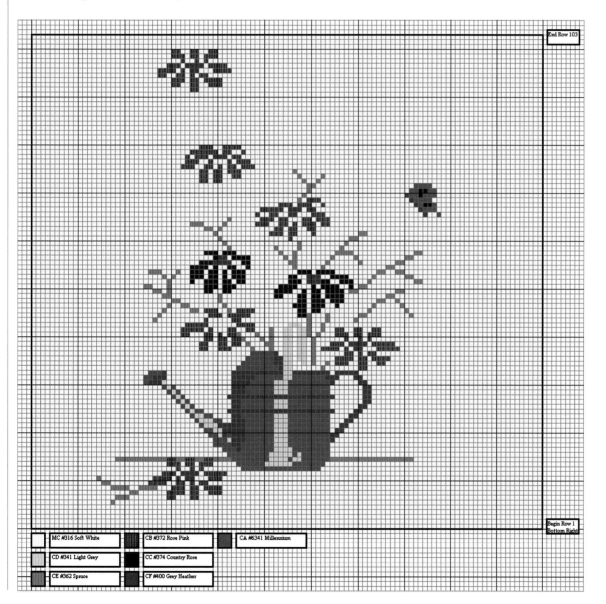

	MC #316 Soft White		CB #372 Rose Pink		CA #6341 Millennium	
	CD #341 Light Grey		CC #374 Country Rose			
	CE #362 Spruce		CF #400 Grey Heather			

country blue

(continued from page 64)

Rnd 2 Join A in 2nd sc of any corner, ch 3 (count as 1 dc), work (1 dc, ch 2, 2 dc) in same joining st, *[sk 1 st, 2 dc in next st] rep between []'s up to next corner sc, work (2 dc, ch 2, 2 dc) in corner st; rep from * twice, rep between []'s to next corner. Join with a sl st to beg ch. Do not turn.

Rnds 3 and 4 Sl st up to ch-2 sp, ch 3, (count as 1 dc), work (1 dc, ch 2, 2 dc) in same ch-sp, *[sk next dc, 2 dc in sp between next 2 dc], rep between []'s to next corner, work (2 dc, ch 2, 2 dc) in corner ch-2 sp; rep from * twice, rep between []'s to next corner. Join with sl st to beg ch. Do not turn. At the end of rnd 4 join C. Do not turn.

Rnd 5 Ch 2, hdc in each dc, 4 hdc in each ch-2 sps. Join with a sl st to beg ch. Turn.

Rnd 6 Join A, ch 2, hdc around post of each hdc with no incs all around. Join with a sl st to beg ch. Turn.

Rnd 7 Join C, rep rnd 5.

Rnd 8 Rep rnd 6. At the end of rnd 8, fasten off A. Turn.

Rnd 9 Join B, 1 sc in each hdc, 3 sc in each corner. Fasten off.

finishing

Join in rows of 3 squares by 4.

Edging

From RS, join B in any corner. **Rnd 1** Ch 1, 1 sc in each sc all around, working 3 sc in each corner sc, end 2 sc in joining st, sl st in beg ch. Do not turn. **Rnd 2** Working from left to right, sc in each st around. Fasten off.

pillow

Work 1 square motif. Attach square to a 16"/40.5cm blue pillow.

prairie star

(continued from page 68)

assembly chart

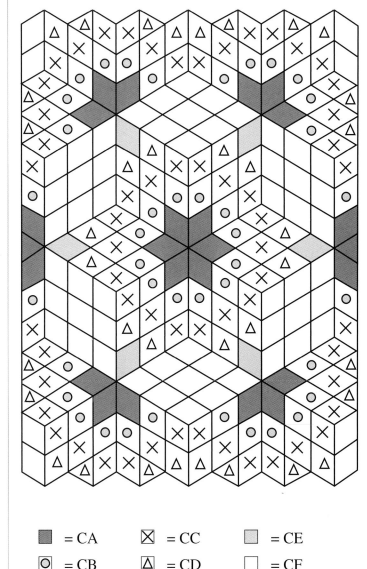

■ = CA		⊠ = CC		▨ = CE	
◉ = CB		△ = CD		□ = CF	

patchwork cross afghan

(continued from page 72)

Border

With RS facing and crochet hook, join B in upper RH corner sc. **Rnd 1** Ch 1, hdc in each st around (count joining seam as 2 sts), work (hdc, ch 2 hdc) in each corner ch-2 sp. Join rnd with a sl st in beg hdc. **Rnd 2** Ch 1, hdc in each hdc around, work (hdc, ch 2, hdc) in each corner ch-2 sp. Join rnd with a sl st in beg hdc. Fasten off. **Rnd 3** With RS, join C in upper RH corner hdc, ch 1, hdc in corner hdc, hdc in each of next 2 hdc, *ch 1, sk next hdc, **hdc in each of next 3 hdc*; rep from * across to within 2 hdc from corner; ch 1, sk next hdc, hdc in next hdc, work (hdc, ch 2, hdc) in corner ch-2 sp**; rep from ** to ** 3 times more. Join rnd with a sl st in beg hdc. Fasten off. **Rnd 4** With RS facing, join A in upper RH corner hdc, ch 1, hdc in corner hdc, hdc in each of next 3 hdc, dc in next corresponding hdc 2 rnds below (rnd 2) pulling dc up to current level of work, *hdc in each of next 3 hdc, dc in next corresponding hdc 2 rnds below (rnd 2), pulling dc up to current level of work*; rep from * to * across to within 2 hdc from corner ch-2 sp, hdc in each of next 2 hdc, work (hdc, ch 2, hdc) in corner ch-2 sp, **hdc in each of next 4 hdc, dc in next corresponding hdc 2 rnds below (rnd 2); rep from ** to ** twice more. Join rnd with a sl st in beg hdc. Fasten off. **Rnd 5** With RS facing, join B in upper RH corner hdc, ch 1, hdc in each of first 5 hdc, *ch 1, sk next dc, hdc in each of next 3 hdc*; rep from * to * across to next corner ch-2 sp, work (hdc, ch 2, hdc) in corner ch-2 sp, **hdc in each of next 5 hdc; rep from * to * across to next corner ch-2 sp, work (hdc, ch 2, hdc) in corner ch-2 sp**; rep from ** to ** twice more. Join rnd with a sl st in beg hdc. Fasten off. **Rnd 6** With RS facing, join A in upper RH corner ch-2 sp, **8 dc in corner ch-2 sp, sk next 3 hdc, sc in next hdc, sk next 2 hdc, 8 dc in next ch-1 sp, sk next 3 hdc, sc in next ch-1 sp*; rep from * to * across to within 4 hdc from corner ch-2 sp, sk next 4 hdc**; rep from ** to ** 3 times more. Join rnd with a sl st in beg sc. Fasten off. **Rnd 7** Ch 1, sc in each st around. Join rnd with a sl st in beg sc. Fasten off.

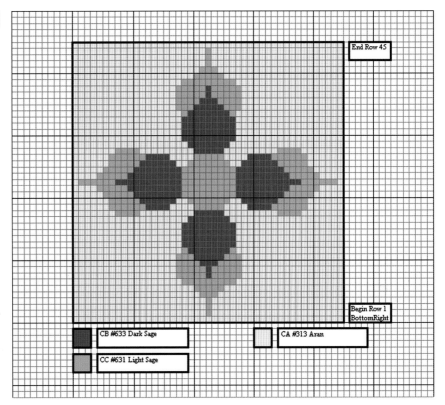

End Row 45

Begin Row 1 Bottom Right

CB #633 Dark Sage

CA #313 Aran

CC #631 Light Sage

retro chic

satin granny squares

(continued from page 76)

finishing

Join 9 motifs wide by 11 motifs long.

Tassel

(make 4)

Wind A around cardboard 30 times. Cut yarn leaving a long end and thread end through yarn needle. Sl needle through all lps and tie tightly. Remove cardboard and wind yarn tightly around loops 1"/2.5cm below fold. Fasten securely. Cut through rem lps and trim ends evenly. Sew a tassel to each corner.

amish blocks

(continued from page 78)

afghan

Foll diagram as indicated, matching all sides and corners, and inserting half-motifs where appropriate.

finishing

Border

Row 1 (RS) Join MC in any corner, ch 1, *work (sc, ch 3, sc) in corner, [ch 1, sk 1 st, sl st in next st] to next corner, (**Note** It may be necessary to sk more than 1 st on occasion to make sure work lays flat); rep from * 3 times; end sl st to first sc, sl st in ch-3 sp, ch 2. Turn. **Row 2** *Work 3 hdc in ch-3 sp, [2 hdc in ch-1 sp] to next corner, 3 hdc in ch-3 sp, ch 3; rep from * 3 times. Join with a sl st in 2nd ch of ch-2. Fasten off. Turn. **Row 3** Join A in any corner, working in back lps only, ch 3 , 2 dc in same sp, *ch 3, work 3 dc in same corner; dc in each hdc to corner, work 3 dc in corner; rep from * 3 times, ending last rep with ch 1, hdc in 3rd ch of first ch-3, ch 1. Turn. **Row 4** Sl st in corner sp, ch 2, hdc in corner sp, *hdc in front lp of each dc to corner**, work (2 hdc, ch 2, hdc) in corner sp; rep from * twice, then from * to ** once, in last corner, work 2 hdc, ch 2, sl st in 2nd ch of ch-2. Fasten off. Turn. **Row 5** Join B in any corner sp. Rep row 3. **Row 6** Rep row 1. Do not turn. **Row 7** Sc in front lp of each hdc around, (**Note** If work gets too bulky, change to a smaller hook). Fasten off.

christmas rose

(continued from page 86)

previous strip as before. Join second and subsequent motifs to side of previous motif and to side of motif of the previous strip; as motifs are joined on alternate sides, a square opening is formed; see diagram. Make 6 strips of 8 motifs.

square filler motif

(make 35)

With B, ch 4. Join with sl st to form a ring.

Rnd 1 Ch 1, work 8 sc in ring. Join with a sl st in first sc. Fasten off.

Rnd 2 Join D in any sc, work (beg cluster, ch 2, Cl) all in first sc, *ch 4**, sk 1 sc, work (sl, ch 2, Cl) all in next sc; rep from * around, end at **. Join with a sl st in top of beg Cl. Fasten off.

Rnd 3 Rep rnd 8 of flower motif.

Rnd 4 Ch 1, work (sc, ch 1, sc) all in first sc, *ch 1, sk next sc, [sc in next sc, ch 1, sk next sc] 4 times**, work (sc, ch 1, sc) all in next sc; rep from * around, end at **. Join. Fasten off.

Rnd 5 Rep rnd 10 of flower motif.

Rnd 6 Rep rnd 11 of second flower motif joining all 4 sides in square area between motifs.

finishing

Border

Rnd 1 With RS facing join C in any ch-3 corner sp, ch 1, *work (sc, ch 3, sc) in corner sp, ch 3, [sc in ch-3 sp, ch 3] 3 times; rep from * around working dec at joinings as foll: insert hook in joined ch-3 corner sp of first motif and pull lp through, insert hook in sl st of joining and pull lp through, insert hook in joined ch-3 corner sp of next motif and pull lp through; yo and draw through all 4 lps on hook. Join with a sl st in first sc.

Rnd 2 Sl st in ch-3 sp, ch 1, *(sc, ch 1, sc) in corner, ch 2, [sc in ch-3 sp, ch 2] 4 times; rep from * around except work ch 1 over dec instead of ch 2. Join. Fasten off.

Rnd 3 Join E in any corner ch-1 sp, ch 1, **work (sc, ch 1, sc) in corner sp, ch 2, *[sc in ch 2 sp, ch

2]; rep from * to corner; rep from ** around. Join.

Rnd 4 Sl st in ch-sp, *work (beg puff st, ch 1, ps) in corner ch-1 sp, ch 1, [ps in next ch-2 sp, ch 1] 6 times; rep from * around except work (ps, ch 1, ps) in each corner and work sts in brackets 4 times before and after each dec area sk ch-2 over dec. Join. Fasten off.

Rnd 5 Join C in any corner ch-1sp, ch 1, *(sc, ch 1, sc) in corner, ch 1, [sc in next ch-1 sp, ch 1] 7 times; rep from * around except sk ch-1 at dec

area and work sts in brackets 4 times before and after this area. Join.

Rnd 6 Sl st in ch-sp, ch 1, *(sc, ch 3, sc) in corner, ch 1, sc in next sc, ch 1, [(sc, ch 3, sc) all in next sc, ch 1, sc in next sc, ch 1] 3 times; rep from * around except work sts in brackets once to dec area, sk next (ch 1 and sc), work (sc, ch 3, sc) in ch-1 sp over dec area, sk next (sc and ch 1), sc in next sc, ch 1, work sts in brackets once to corner. Join. Fasten off.

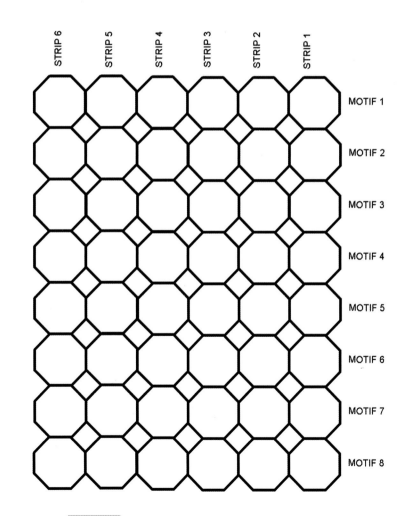

STRIP 6 STRIP 5 STRIP 4 STRIP 3 STRIP 2 STRIP 1

MOTIF 1
MOTIF 2
MOTIF 3
MOTIF 4
MOTIF 5
MOTIF 6
MOTIF 7
MOTIF 8

airplane blanket

(continued from page 94)

Top and bottom edging

From RS, with circular needle and E, pick up and k 175 sts evenly spaced along top edge. Knit next 2 rows. Bind off knitwise. Rep along bottom edge.

Side edging

From RS, with circular needle and C, pick up and k 213 sts evenly spaced along side edge. Knit next 2 rows. Bind off knitwise. Rep along opposite edge.

Chart I

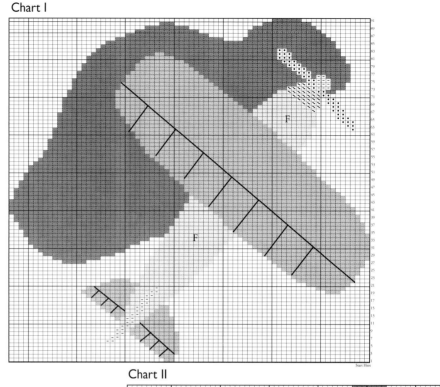

Key for Chart I

☐ = MC (Lt. Blue)

▨ = Contrast A (Winter White)

▨ = Contrast B (Cardinal)

◲ = Contrast D (Gold)

☐ = Contrast F (Copen Blue)

⊡ = Contrast G (Aqua Sea)

⊟ = Contrast H (Navy)

╱ = straight st with H (Navy)

Chart II

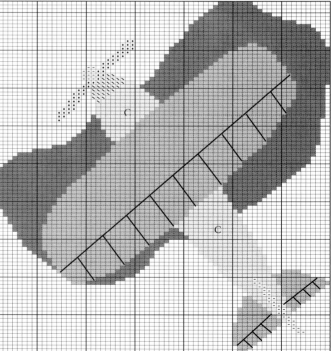

Key for Chart II

☐ = MC (Lt. Blue)

▨ = Contrast A (Winter White)

◲ = Contrast B (Cardinal)

☐ = Contrast C (Mauve)

▨ = Contrast E (Bright Royal)

⊡ = Contrast G (Aqua Sea)

⊟ = Contrast H (Navy)

╱ = straight st with G (Aqua Sea)

Chart III

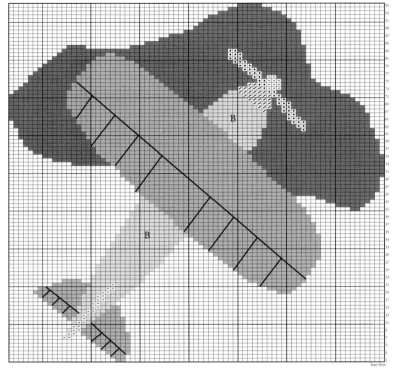

Key for Chart III

☐ = MC (Lt. Blue)

■ = Contrast A (Winter White)

☐ = Contrast B (Cardinal)

◪ = Contrast C (Mauve)

▨ = Contrast D (Gold)

⊡ = Contrast G (Aqua Sea)

⊟ = Contrast H (Navy)

╱ = straight st with H (Navy)

airplane toy

(continued from page 144)

materials

*Canadiana by Patons®, 3½oz/100g balls,
each approx 201yd/184m (acrylic)
1 ball each in #30 med blue (MC),
#32 bright royal (B)
Small amounts of #26 mauve (A),
#34 navy (C), #5 cardinal (D)
and #81 gold (E)*

---

*One pair size 6 (4mm) needles
OR SIZE TO OBTAIN GAUGE*

Yarn needle

Polyester fiberfill

intermediate

finished measurements

13" x 13"/33 x 33 cm

gauge

21 sts and 27 rows to 4"/10cm over St st using size 6 (4mm) needles.
TAKE TIME TO CHECK YOUR GAUGE

body

With MC, cast on 10 sts.
Row 1 (RS) *Inc 1 st in next st; rep from * to end—20 sts.
Row 2 and all WS rows Purl.
Row 3 *K1, inc 1 st in next st; rep from * to end—30 sts.
Next 3 rows Work in St st.
Row 7 *K2, inc 1 st in next st; rep from * to end—40 sts. Beg with a p row, work even in St st for 15 rows. With B, work even in St st for 30 rows. With MC, work even in St st for 8 rows.
Front shaping
Row 1 (RS) With E, *k2, k2tog; rep from * to end—30 sts.
Row 2 and all WS rows Purl.
Row 3 With A, *k1, k2tog; rep from * to end—20 sts.
Row 5 *K2tog; rep from * to end—10 sts.
Row 6 Purl. Cut yarn leaving a 12"/30.5cm long tail. Thread tail in yarn needle and weave through rem sts. Pull tight to gather, then fasten off securely. Sew bottom seam leaving an opening for stuffing. Stuff body; sew opening closed.

wing

(make 2)
With B, cast on 40 sts. Work even in St st for 4 rows. Dec 1 st each side on next row, then every other row 12 times more—14 sts. Bind off. Fold wing along center of work and sew to cast-on edge. Sew side edges tog. Stuff wings and sew cast-on edge to sides of body; as shown.

airplane toy

(continued from page 145)

tail

With B, cast on 30 sts. Work even in St st for 4 rows. Dec 1 st each side on next row, then every 4th row 7 times more—14 sts. Bind off. Fold tail along center of work and sew to bound-off edge. Sew side edges tog. Stuff tail and sew cast-on edge to top back of body; as shown.

tail detail

(make 2)

With D, cast on 12 sts.

Row 1 (WS) Knit.

Row 2 [P2tog] 6 times—6 sts. Cut yarn leaving a long tail. Thread tail in yarn needle, then weave through rem sts. Pull tight to gather, then fasten off securely. Sew seam. Sew to sides of tail; as shown.

nose

With C, cast on 20 sts loosely.

Row 1 (WS) Knit.

Row 2 [P2tog] 10 times—10 sts. Cut yarn leaving a long tail. Thread tail in yarn needle, then weave through rem sts. Pull tight to gather, then fasten off securely. Sew seam. Sew to front of body leaving an opening for stuffing. Stuff nose lightly, then sew opening closed.

propeller

(make 2)

With C, cast on 20 sts loosely.

Row 1 (WS) K14, turn (leave rem sts unworked).

Row 2 Knit. Bind off all sts. Sew pieces to nose; as shown.

STRAIGHT STITCH

quilted squares

(continued from page 100)

motif III

(make 7)

Work as given for motif I, using C instead of A.

finishing

Referring to diagram, sew motifs into strips, then sew strips into blanket.

Edging

Rnd 1 Join MC with a sl st in top right corner, ch 3, work 4 dc in same sp, working in back lp only of each st to end of rnd, *1 dc in each st across to next corner, work 5 dc in next corner; rep from * twice more, end 1 dc in each st across to first corner. Join with a sl st in 3rd ch of ch-3. **Rnds 2 and 3** Ch 3, 1 dc in each dc across to next corner dc, *5 dc in next corner dc, 1 dc in each dc across to next corner dc; rep from * 3 times more. Join with a sl st in 3rd ch of ch-3. After rnd 3 is completed, fasten off. **Rnd 4** Join A with sl st in first corner dc, ch 3, work 4 dc in same sp, *1 dc in each dc across to next corner dc, 5 dc in next corner dc; rep from * twice more, end 1 dc in each dc across to first corner. Join with a sl st in 3rd ch of ch-3. **Rnd 5** Working from left to right, work 1 sc in each dc around (see illustrations). Join with a sl st in first sc. Fasten off.

easy as 1-2-3

(continued from page 104)

ing motif I and motif II. For side, sew 13 motifs tog, alternating motif II and motif I. Do not sew to blanket.

Inner edging

With hook, join MC with a sl st in first motif of bottom left corner of border granny square border, ch 1, *work 1 sc in each of next 9 dc across first motif, work 1 sc in joining sp between 2 motifs; rep from * to next corner. Dec in corner as foll: draw up a lp in corner 2 dc, yo and draw through all 3 lps on hook (sc 2tog made); ** rep from * to ** around, working sc 2tog across last and first sc. Join with a sl st in first sc.

Fasten off.

Outer edging

With hook, join MC with a sl st in any corner, ch 1, work 1 sc in each of next 9 dc across first motif, *work 1 sc in joining sp between 2 motifs, work 1 sc in each of next 9 dc across next motif; rep from * around, working 3 sc in each corner. Join with a sl st in first sc. Fasten off. Sew granny square border to center section.

wee granny squares

(continued from page 108)

ch-1 sp] to corner, in corner ch-3 sp work (ch 1, 3 dc, ch 3, 3 dc); rep from * around, end work (ch 1, 3 dc, ch 3) in first corner. Join rnd with a sl st in top of beg ch-3. Turn.

Row 1 (WS) Sl st in ch-3 sp, in first dc work sl st, ch 4 (counts as 1 dc and ch 1, [work 3 dc in next ch-1 sp, ch 1] across 44 times, sk 2 dc, dc in next dc until 2 lps rem on hook, with A yo and complete the dc (color change made). Turn. Fasten off E.

Row 2 With A, ch 3 (counts as 1 dc), 2 dc in first sp, (ch 1, sk 3 dc, 3 dc in next sp) 44 times; turn.

Row 3 With A, ch 4 (counts as 1 dc and ch 1), [work 3 dc in next ch-1 sp, ch 1] 44 times, sk 2 dc, dc in next dc changing to B. Turn. Fasten off A.

Rows 4-5 With B, rep rows 2-3 changing to C at the end of row 5. Fasten off B.

Rows 6-7 With C, rep rows 2-3 changing to D at the end of 7ow 7. Fasten off C.

Rows 8-9 With D, rep rows 2-3 changing to E at the end of row 9. Fasten off D.

Rows 10-11 With E, rep rows 2-3. After row 11, fasten off E ***.

Rep from *** to *** for second set of 5 granny squares in first color sequence. Join tog 5 squares of second color sequence. Using second strip in the center, join one of the first strips to the side edge so that the colors from left to right on first are E, D, C, B, A and E. Join rem first strip to second so that the colors from right to left are E, D, C, B, A and E.

Edging

With RS facing, join E with a sl st in any corner.

Rnd 1 Ch 3 (counts as 1 dc), in same sp work (2 dc, ch 3, 3 dc), *ch 1, work 3 dc in next sp; rep from * around working (ch 1, 3 dc, ch 3, 3 dc) in each corner, end ch 1. Join rnd with a sl st in top of beg ch-3.

Rnd 2 Sl st to corner ch-3 sp, then rep rnd 1.

Rnd 3 Ch 1, sc in joining and in each of next 2 dc. Working 5 sc in each corner ch-3 sp, sc in each dc and ch-1 sp around. Join rnd with a sl st in first sc.

Rnd 4 Ch 3 (counts as 1 dc), dc in each sc around working 3 dc in 3rd sc of each corner. Join rnd with a sl st in top of beg ch-3. Turn.

Rnd 5 (WS) Ch 1, sc in each dc around working 3 sc in 2nd dc of each corner. Join rnd with a sl st in first sc. Fasten off.

clustered bobbles

(continued from page 110)

combination) to any ch-1 sp, ch 6 (counts as 1 dc and ch-3 base for cluster), work Cl st in 3rd ch from hook, ch 1, *sc in next ch-1 sp, ch 1, dc in next ch-1 sp, ch 3, work Cl st in 3rd ch from hook, ch 1 **; rep from * to ** around. Join with a sl st in 3rd ch of ch-6. Fasten off.

assembly chart

1	2	1	2	1	2	1	2	1	2	1	2
2	1	2	1	2	1	2	1	2	1	2	1
1	2	1	2	1	2	1	2	1	2	1	2
2	1	2	1	2	1	2	1	2	1	2	1
1	2	1	2	1	2	1	2	1	2	1	2
2	1	2	1	2	1	2	1	2	1	2	1
1	2	1	2	1	2	1	2	1	2	1	2
2	1	2	1	2	1	2	1	2	1	2	1
1	2	1	2	1	2	1	2	1	2	1	2
2	1	2	1	2	1	2	1	2	1	2	1
1	2	1	2	1	2	1	2	1	2	1	2
2	1	2	1	2	1	2	1	2	1	2	1

cradle comforts

(continued from page 114)

finishing

Sew strips tog, alternating strip A and B; as shown.

Top and bottom edging

With circular needle and MC, pick up and k 153 sts across top edge. **Row 1 (WS)** P1, *k1, p1; rep from * to end. **Row 2** K1, inc 1 st in next st purlwise, *k1, p1; rep from * to last 3 sts, end k1, inc 1 st in next st purlwise, k1. **Row 3** P1, k2, *p1, k1; rep from * to last 3 sts, end k2, p1. **Row 4** K1, inc 1 st in next st purlwise, *p1, k1; rep from * to last 3 sts, end p1, inc 1 st in next st purlwise, k1. Rep rows 1-4 until edging measures 2"/5cm from beg, end with a WS row. Bind off loosely in rib. Rep along bottom edge.

Side edging

With circular needle and MC, pick up and knit 185 sts along side edge. Work same as for top and bottom edging. Rep along opposite side edge. Sew edging tog at corners.

Chart I

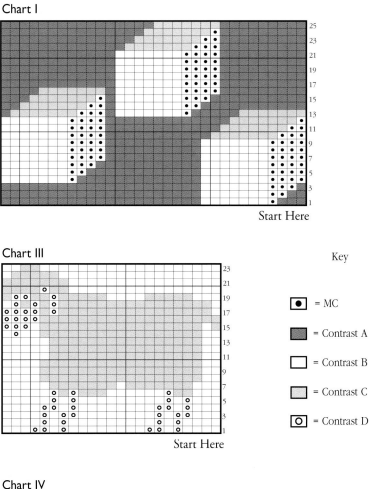

Start Here

Chart III

Key

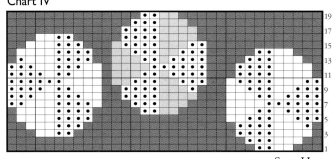

Start Here

Key

- ⬛● = MC
- ⬛ = Contrast A
- ⬜ = Contrast B
- ⬜ = Contrast C
- ⬜○ = Contrast D

Chart II

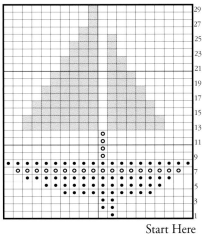

Start Here

Chart IV

Start Here

counting sheep

(continued from page 116)

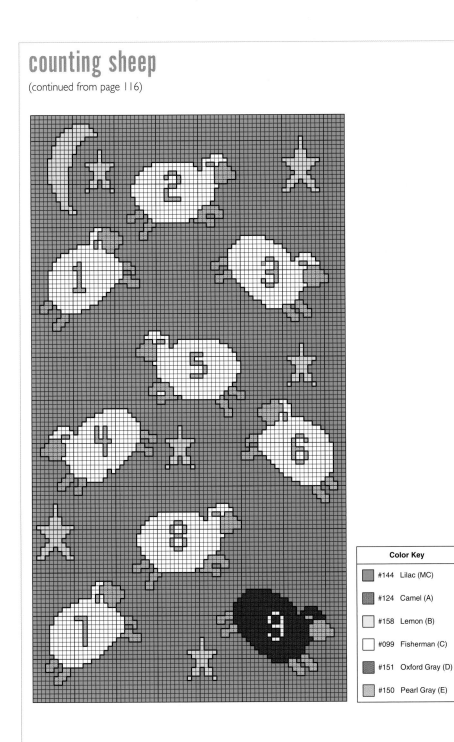

Color Key	
■	#144 Lilac (MC)
▨	#124 Camel (A)
▢	#158 Lemon (B)
▢	#099 Fisherman (C)
▨	#151 Oxford Gray (D)
▨	#150 Pearl Gray (E)

autumn treasure

(continued from page 120)

using D instead of MC.

Small square 4
(make 2 for each block A)
Work as for small square 1 until last rnd and using E instead of MC.

Assembling
Assemble squares as shown in diagram to form block A. From RS, join B in top right corner and work 1 rnd of sc around outer edge, working 3 sc in each corner. Join with sl st to first sc. Fasten off.

block B

(make 15)
Note To change color, work to last 2 lps on hook. Draw loop in next color through 2 lps on hook to complete st and proceed in next color. With E, ch 42 loosely.

Foundation row (RS) Dc in 4th ch from hook, 1 dc in each of next 2 ch, *with B, 1 dc in each of next 4 ch, with E, 1 dc in each of next 4 ch; rep from * twice more, with B, 1 dc in each of last 4 ch, 40 dc. Ch 3, turn.

Row 1 Sk first dc, 1 dc in each of next 3 dc, *with E, 1 dc in each of next 4 dc, with B, 1 dc in each of next 4 dc; rep from * twice more, with E, 1 dc in each of next 4 dc. With D, ch 3, turn.

Row 2 Sk first dc, 1 dc in each of next 3 dc, *with D, 1 dc in each of next 4 dc, with B, 1 dc in each of next 4 dc; rep from * twice more, with D, 1 dc in each of next 4 dc. Ch 3, turn.

Row 3 Sk first dc, 1 dc in each of next 3 dc, *with B, 1 dc in each of next 4 dc, with D, 1 dc in each of next 4 dc; rep from * twice more, with B, 1 dc in each of next 4 dc. With E, ch 3, turn.

Row 4 Sk first dc, 1 dc in each of next 3 dc, *with C, 1 dc in each of next 4 dc, with E, 1 dc in each of next 4 dc; rep from * twice more, with C, 1 dc in each of next 4 dc. Ch 3, turn.

Row 5 Sk first dc, 1 dc in each of next 3 dc, *with E, 1 dc in each of next 4 dc, with C, 1 dc in each of next 4 dc; rep from * twice more, with E, 1 dc in each of next 4 dc. With C, ch 3, turn.

autumn treasure

(continued from page 149)

Row 6 Sk first dc, 1 dc in each of next 3 dc, *with D, 1 dc in each of next 4 dc, with C, 1 dc in each of next 4 dc; rep from * twice more, with D, 1 dc in each of next 4 dc. Ch 3, turn.
Row 7 Sk first dc, 1 dc in each of next 3 dc, *with C, 1 dc in each of next 4 dc, with D, 1 dc in each of next 4 dc; rep from * twice more, with C, 1 dc in each of next 4 dc. With E, ch 3, turn.
Row 8 Sk first dc, 1 dc in each of next 3 dc, *with B, 1 dc in each of next 4 dc, with E, 1 dc in each of next 4 dc; rep from * twice more, with B, 1 dc in each of next 4 dc. Ch 3, turn. Rep rows 1-8 once more, then row 1 once omitting turning ch at end of last row. Fasten off.

finishing

Assemble blocks A and B as shown in diagram II.
Edging
Rnd 1 With RS facing, join B with a sl st in any corner, ch 1, work 3 sc in same sp, cont to sc evenly around, working 3 sc in each corner. Join MC with sl st in first sc. Cut B. **Rnd 2** Ch 1, sc in each sc around, working 3 sc in corner sc. Join with sl st in first sc. **Rnd 3** Ch 1, working from left to right, work 1 sc in each sc around (see illustrations below). Join with sl st in first sc. Fasten off.

Block A

Large Square		Small Square 1	Small Square 2
Large Square		Small Square 3	Small Square 4
Small Square 1	Small Square 2	Large Square	
Small Square 3	Small Square 4	Large Square	

A	B	A	B	A
B	A	B	A	B
A	B	A	B	A
B	A	B	A	B
A	B	A	B	A
B	A	B	A	B

commemorative police thro

(continued from page 124)

strips to motifs. Use long strips to connect three panels.

finishing
Top and bottom borders
From RS with circular needle and MC, pick up and k 188 sts along top of afghan. Work in rib pat for 6 rows, inc 1 st each side every other row 2 times—192 sts. Bind off in rib pat. Rep for bottom of afghan.
Side borders
From RS with circular needle and MC, pick up and k 276 sts along side of afghan. Work in rib pat same as top border—280 sts. Bind off in rib pat. Sew corner seams.
Whistle cord
With MC and crochet hook, make a chain st cord following photo for placement.

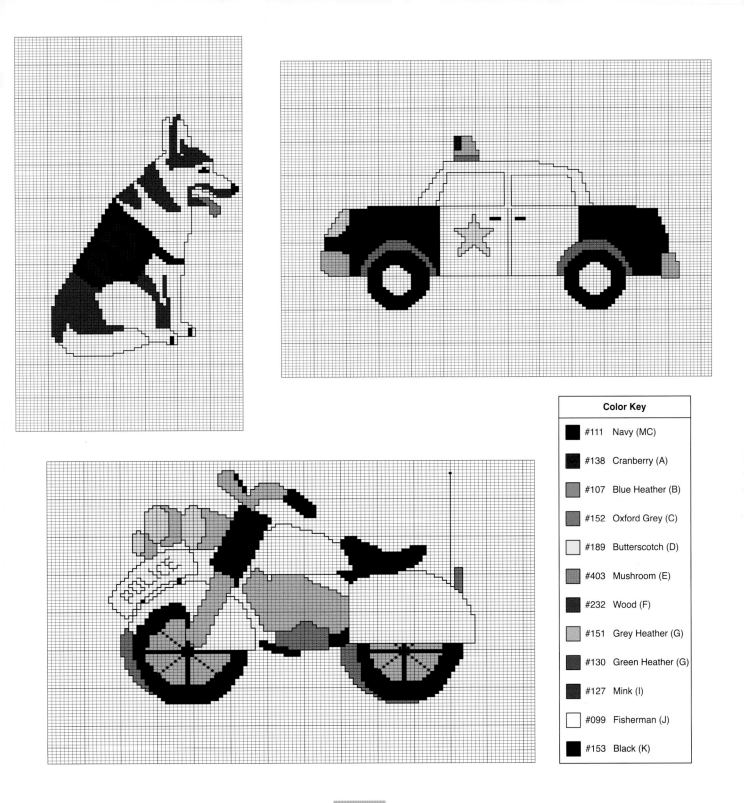

Color Key

■	#111	Navy (MC)
■	#138	Cranberry (A)
■	#107	Blue Heather (B)
■	#152	Oxford Grey (C)
□	#189	Butterscotch (D)
■	#403	Mushroom (E)
■	#232	Wood (F)
■	#151	Grey Heather (G)
■	#130	Green Heather (G)
■	#127	Mink (I)
□	#099	Fisherman (J)
■	#153	Black (K)

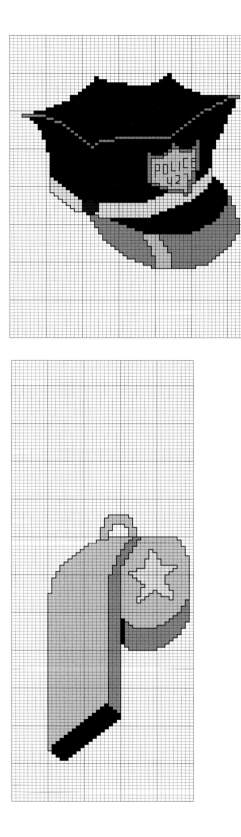

commemorative fireman throw

(continued from page 126)

embroidery

Working in cross stitch, embroider all panels by centering charts for motif and working in colors as indicated.

vertical panels

Work all panels with D.

Bottom

With afghan hook, ch 9 and work 52 rows BAS. Sew between Fireman's Hat and Fire Hose panels.

Middle

(make 2)

With afghan hook, ch 9 and work 104 rows BAS, sew one between Fire Hydrant and Firehouse, the other between Firehouse and Dalmation panels.

Top

With afghan hook, ch 9 and work 70 rows BAS. Sew between Firetruck and Fire Alarm panels.

horizontal panels

Work all panels with D.

Top

With afghan hook, pick up 194 sts and work 9 rows BAS.

Middle

With afghan hook, pick up 194 sts and work 9 rows BAS. Sew to top panel.

Bottom

With afghan hook, pick up 194 sts and work 9 rows BAS. Sew to middle panel. Rotate afghan and pick up 194 sts across bottom edge. Work 9 rows BAS.

finishing

Edging

With crochet hook, sc evenly around afghan, working 3 sc in each corner. **Picot Row** *Work 5 sc, ch 3, sl st into top of last sc; rep from *, working 3 sc in each corner.

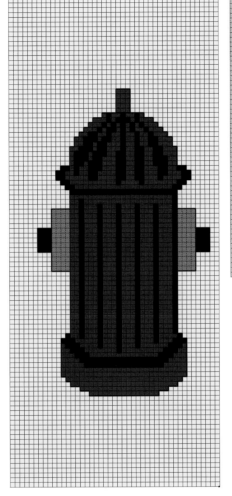

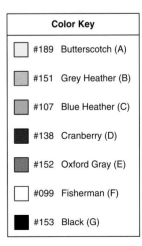

Color Key	
#189	Butterscotch (A)
#151	Grey Heather (B)
#107	Blue Heather (C)
#138	Cranberry (D)
#152	Oxford Gray (E)
#099	Fisherman (F)
#153	Black (G)

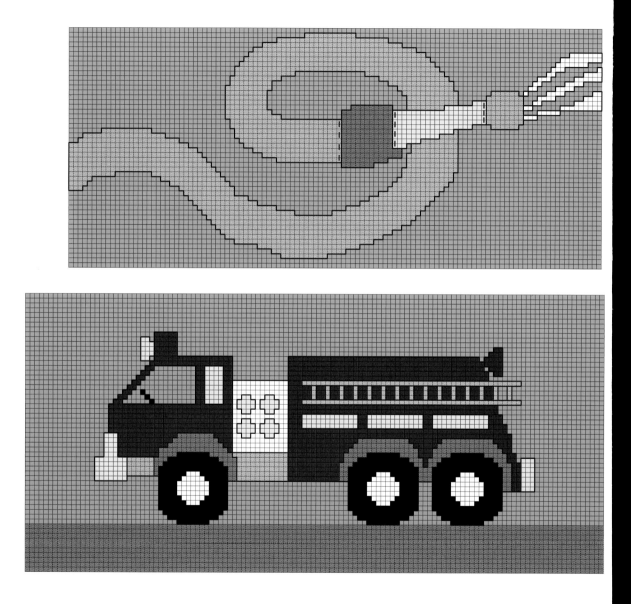

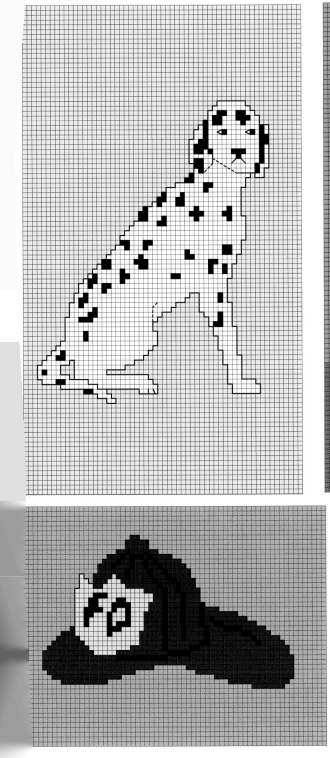

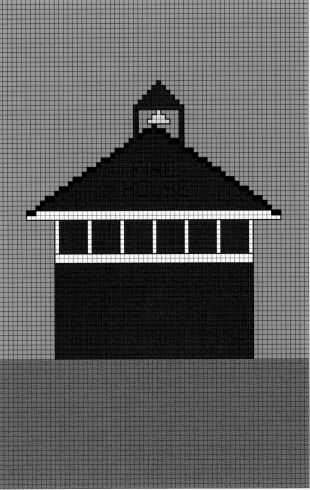

country santa

(continued from page 128)

Border

With RS facing, using size crochet hook, join C in upper right corner st. **Rnd 1** Ch 1, sc evenly spaced around, working a ch 1 around each corner. Join rnd with a sl st in beg sc. Fasten off.

Block B

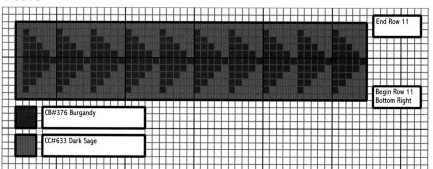

End Row 11

Begin Row 11
Bottom Right

| | CB#376 Burgandy |
| | CC#633 Dark Sage |

Block C

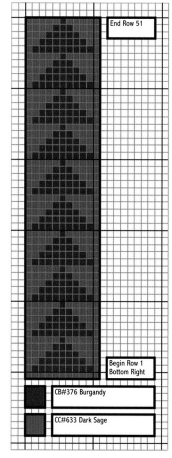

End Row 51

Begin Row 1
Bottom Right

| | CB#376 Burgandy |
| | CC#633 Dark Sage |

Block D

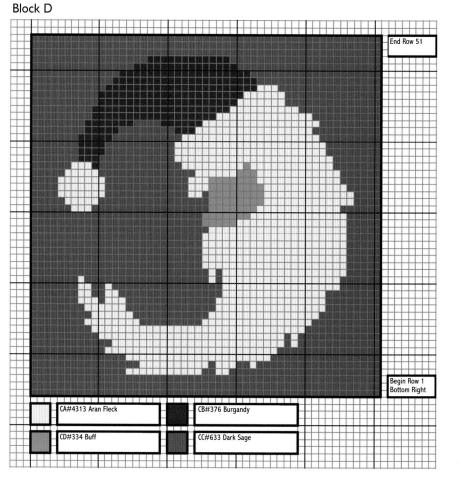

End Row 51

Begin Row 1
Bottom Right

| | CA#4313 Aran Fleck | | CB#376 Burgandy |
| | CD#334 Buff | | CC#633 Dark Sage |

assembly diagram

A	B	A	B	A	B	A
C	D SANTA	C	E PLAIN	C	D SANTA	C
A	B	A	B	A	B	A
C	E PLAIN	C	D SANTA	C	E PLAIN	C
A	B	A	B	A	B	A
C	D SANTA	C	E PLAIN	C	D SANTA	C
A	B	A	B	A	B	A

Cross Stitch Chart

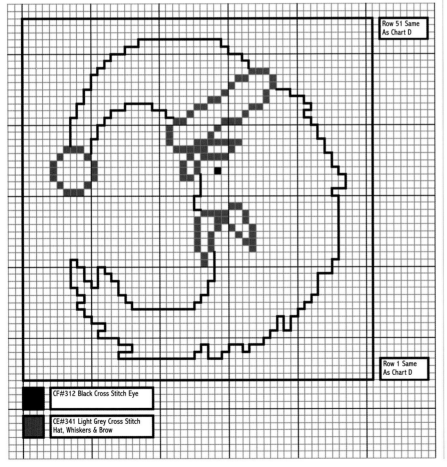

Row 51 Same As Chart D

Row 1 Same As Chart D

CF#312 Black Cross Stitch Eye

CE#341 Light Grey Cross Stitch Hat, Whiskers & Brow

falling leaves
(continued from page 130)

panel in this manner taking care to keep panel in same direction.

finishing

Border

Rnd 1 Using color of your choice, join yarn in any corner, ch 1, sc, ch-3, sc in same corner, *ch 1, sl 1 st, sc in next st; rep from * around working (sc, ch 3, sc) for each corner. Join with a sl st in first sc. **Rnd 2** Rep rnd 1, working sc in ch-1 sp of previous rnd, ch-1 over sc. **Rnd 3** Join A in any corner, ch 1, work (sc, ch 3, sc) all in same sp, *sc in next ch-1 sp, ch 3; rep from * around, working (sc, ch 3, sc) in corner. Join. Fasten off.

summer shells

(continued from page 132)

2 hdc, *ch 2, sk 2 hdc, dc in next 2 hdc; rep from * around. Join in 3rd ch of ch-3. Fasten off. **Rnd 3** Join A with a sl st in any dc, sc in next dc, *(dc in each of 2 sk hdc of previous rnd, sc in next 2 dc) to next corner, 3 dc in center st of 3-hdc corner; rep from * around. Joing in first sc. Fasten off. **Rnd 4** Join MC in any st with a sl st, hdc evenly spaced around, working 3 hdc in each corner. Join rnd with a sl st in first hdc. **Rnd 5** *Ch 2, 2 dc in same st, sk 2 hdc, sl st in next st; rep from * around. Join in first ch of ch-2. Fasten off.

Chart 1

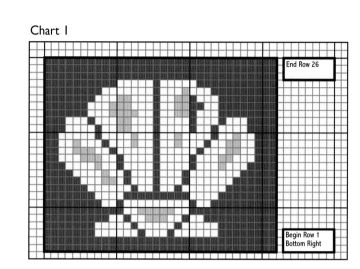

Chart 4

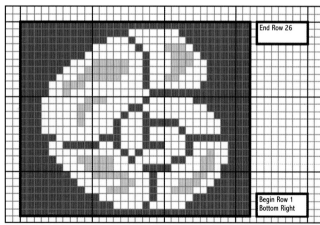

Chart 5

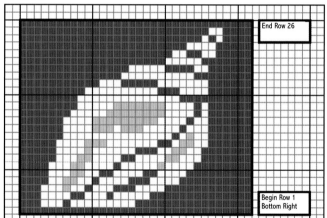

Chart 2

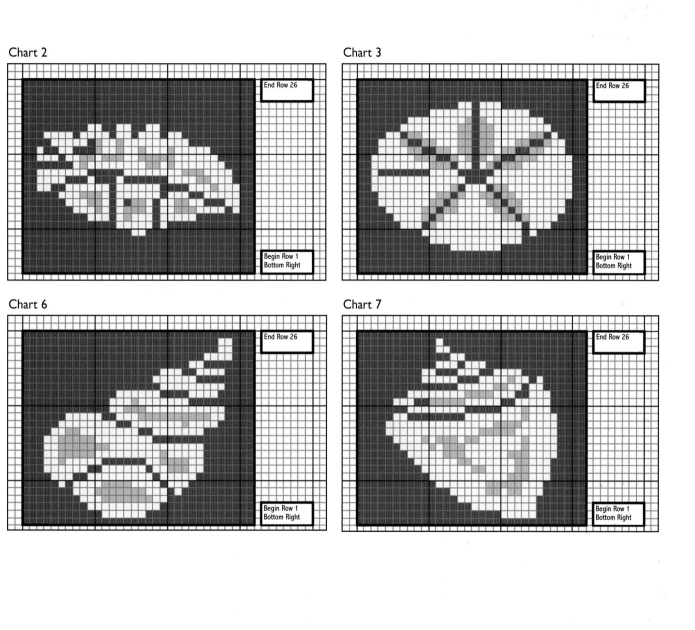

End Row 26

Begin Row 1
Bottom Right

Chart 3

End Row 26

Begin Row 1
Bottom Right

Chart 6

End Row 26

Begin Row 1
Bottom Right

Chart 7

End Row 26

Begin Row 1
Bottom Right

MC#316 Soft White

CB#6301 Baby White

CA#382 Country Blue

yarn resources

All yarns are available and current at the time publishing. For more information about the yarns or to locate a store near you, please visit the following websites.

Bernat®
PO Box 40
Listowel, ON N4W 3H3
Canada
www.bernat.com

Caron® International
Attn: Consumer Service
P.O. Box 222
Washington, NC 27889
www.caron.com

Coats & Clark™
Attn: Consumer Service
P.O. Box 12229
Greenville, SC 29612-0229
www.coatscna.com

Lion Brand Yarns
34 West 15th Street
New York, NY 10011
www.lionbrand.com

Patons®
PO Box 40
Listowel, ON N4W 3H3
Canada
www.patonsyarns.com

In Canada
Coats & Clark™ Canada
6060 Burnside Court
Unit 2
Mississauga, ON L5T 2T5

acknowledgments

We'd like to thank all the people who have contributed to the making of this book. First and foremost, thank you to all the yarn companies—Bernat®, Caron®, Coats & Clark™, Lion Brand Yarn Company and Patons®—for providing these beautiful afghans and throws. We'd like to extend our gratitude to Sara Arblaster, Svetlana Avrakh, Lynn Carlisle, Judy Hice, Kathleen Sams, Nancy Thomas, and Janet Vetter for all their assistance and support. Special thanks goes to the tireless knitters and contributing technical experts, without whom the book would not be possible.